A Kaleidoscopic View of Chinese Philosophy of Education

This book breaks the stereotype that links Chinese philosophy solely to Confucianism, instead providing a kaleidoscopic view of Chinese philosophy of education. The contributors explore a variety of issues, including the journey of modernisation (or Westernisation) of China's education between the sixteenth and twentieth centuries; Chinese identity and the concept of race in education and history; contemporary interpretations of Confucian pedagogy in relation to twenty-first century skills; the life story of a teacher in modern China as embodying the spirit of a Confucian pedagogue; the ecological self in education; an original interpretation of postmodern-Daoist symbolism; and the role of translation in producing and transmitting knowledge across cultural and linguistic boundaries.

This book was originally published as a special issue of *Educational Philosophy and Theory*.

Ruyu Hung is Professor of Philosophy of Education at the National Chiayi University, Taiwan. She is the author of *Learning Nature* (2010), and *Education between Speech and Writing: Crossing the Boundaries of Dao and Deconstruction* (2017), as well as many philosophical and educational articles.

Educational Philosophy and Theory

Series Editor: Peter Roberts, University of Canterbury, New Zealand

This series is devoted to cutting-edge scholarship in educational philosophy and theory. Each book in the series focuses on a key theme or thinker and includes essays from a range of contributors. To be published in the series, a book will normally have first appeared as a special issue of *Educational Philosophy and Theory*, one of the premier philosophy of education journals in the world. This provides an assurance for readers of the quality of the work and enhances the visibility of the book in the international philosophy of education community. Books in this series combine creativity with rigour and insight. The series is intended to demonstrate the value of diverse theoretical perspectives in educational discourse, and contributors are invited to draw on literature, art and film as well as traditional philosophical sources in their work. Questions of educational policy and practice will also be addressed. The books published in this series will provide key reference points for subsequent theoretical work by other scholars, and will play a significant role in advancing philosophy of education as a field of study.

Titles in the series include:

Education, Ethics and Existence
Camus and the Human Condition
By Peter Roberts, Andrew Gibbons and Richard Heraud

Shifting Focus
Strangers and Strangeness in Literature and Education
Edited by Peter Roberts

Philosophy in Schools
Edited by Felicity Haynes

New Directions in Educational Leadership Theory
Edited by Scott Eacott and Colin W. Evers

Expertise, Pedagogy and Practice
Edited by David Simpson and David Beckett

Philosophy and Pedagogy of Early Childhood
Edited by Sandy Farquhar and E. Jayne White

The Dilemma of Western Philosophy
Edited by Michael A. Peters and Carl Mika

Educational Philosophy and New French Thought
Edited by David R. Cole and Joff P.N. Bradley

Activating Aesthetics
Edited by Elizabeth M. Grierson

Levinas and the Philosophy of Education
Edited by Guoping Zhao

The Confucian Concept of Learning
Revisited for East Asian Humanistic Pedagogies
Edited by Duck-Joo Kwak, Morimichi Kato and Ruyu Hung

A Kaleidoscopic View of Chinese Philosophy of Education
Edited by Ruyu Hung

John Dewey's Democracy and Education in an Era of Globalization
Edited by Mordechai Gordon and Andrea R. English

A Kaleidoscopic View of Chinese Philosophy of Education

Edited by
Ruyu Hung

LONDON AND NEW YORK

First published 2018
by Routledge
2 Park Square, Milton Park, Abingdon, Oxon, OX14 4RN, UK

and by Routledge
711 Third Avenue, New York, NY 10017, USA

Routledge is an imprint of the Taylor & Francis Group, an informa business

© 2018 Philosophy of Education Society of Australasia

All rights reserved. No part of this book may be reprinted or reproduced or utilised in any form or by any electronic, mechanical, or other means, now known or hereafter invented, including photocopying and recording, or in any information storage or retrieval system, without permission in writing from the publishers.

Trademark notice: Product or corporate names may be trademarks or registered trademarks, and are used only for identification and explanation without intent to infringe.

British Library Cataloguing in Publication Data
A catalogue record for this book is available from the British Library

ISBN 13: 978-1-138-48928-8

Typeset in Plantin
by RefineCatch Limited, Bungay, Suffolk

Publisher's Note
The publisher accepts responsibility for any inconsistencies that may have arisen during the conversion of this book from journal articles to book chapters, namely the possible inclusion of journal terminology.

Disclaimer
Every effort has been made to contact copyright holders for their permission to reprint material in this book. The publishers would be grateful to hear from any copyright holder who is not here acknowledged and will undertake to rectify any errors or omissions in future editions of this book.

Contents

Citation Information vii
Notes on Contributors ix

Introduction: Kaleidoscopic View of Chinese Philosophy of Education 1
Ruyu Hung

1. Eastward Expansion of Western Learning: A study of Westernisation of China's modern education by Chinese government overseas-study scholarships 7
Ren-Jie Vincent Lin

2. Learning from the Barbarians? Reflections on Chinese Identity and 'Race' in the Educational Context 22
Hektor K. T. Yan

3. Confucius: Philosopher of twenty-first century skills 37
Leonard Tan

4. Problem-Centered Design and Personal Teaching Style: An exploratory study of Youguang Tu's course on philosophy of education 48
Hongde Lei

5. Towards Self-Realisation: Exploring the ecological self for education 60
Chia-Ling Wang

6. Contextualising Postmodernity in Daoist Symbolism: Toward a mindful education embracing eastern wisdom 70
Rob Blom & Chunlei Lu

7. Translation, the Knowledge Economy, and Crossing Boundaries in Contemporary Education 88
Yun-shiuan (Viola) Chen

Index 103

Citation Information

The chapters in this book were originally published in *Educational Philosophy and Theory*, volume 48, issue 12 (November 2016). When citing this material, please use the original page numbering for each article, as follows:

Guest Editorial
Kaleidoscopic View of Chinese Philosophy of Education
Ruyu Hung
Educational Philosophy and Theory, volume 48, issue 12 (November 2016), pp. 1197–1202

Chapter 1
Eastward Expansion of Western Learning: A study of Westernisation of China's modern education by Chinese government overseas-study scholarships
Ren-Jie Vincent Lin
Educational Philosophy and Theory, volume 48, issue 12 (November 2016), pp. 1203–1217

Chapter 2
Learning from the Barbarians? Reflections on Chinese Identity and 'Race' in the Educational Context
Hektor K.T. Yan
Educational Philosophy and Theory, volume 48, issue 12 (November 2016), pp. 1218–1232

Chapter 3
Confucius: Philosopher of twenty-first century skills
Leonard Tan
Educational Philosophy and Theory, volume 48, issue 12 (November 2016), pp. 1233–1243

Chapter 4
Problem-Centered Design and Personal Teaching Style: An exploratory study of Youguang Tu's course on philosophy of education
Hongde Lei
Educational Philosophy and Theory, volume 48, issue 12 (November 2016), pp. 1244–1255

CITATION INFORMATION

Chapter 5
Towards Self-Realisation: Exploring the ecological self for education
Chia-Ling Wang
Educational Philosophy and Theory, volume 48, issue 12 (November 2016), pp. 1256–1265

Chapter 6
Contextualising Postmodernity in Daoist Symbolism: Toward a mindful education embracing eastern wisdom
Rob Blom & Chunlei Lu
Educational Philosophy and Theory, volume 48, issue 12 (November 2016), pp. 1266–1283

Chapter 7
Translation, the Knowledge Economy, and Crossing Boundaries in Contemporary Education
Yun-shiuan (Viola) Chen
Educational Philosophy and Theory, volume 48, issue 12 (November 2016), pp. 1284–1297

For any permission-related enquiries please visit:
http://www.tandfonline.com/page/help/permissions

Notes on Contributors

Rob Blom holds a Master's degree in Education from Brock University, Canada. His academic interests include postmodern educational trends in complexity theory and deep ecology and postpostmodern (or premodern) educational trends in Eastern Mindfulness, Platonic philosophy, and perennial metaphysics.

Yun-shiuan (Viola) Chen is Assistant Research Fellow at the National Academy for Educational Research, Taiwan. Her research focuses on global studies in education, educational policy analysis and evaluation, as well as philosophy. She is the author of *Modernization or Cultural Imperialism: A Critical Reading for Taiwan's National Scholarship Program for Overseas Study* (2013).

Ruyu Hung is Professor of Philosophy of Education at the National Chiayi University, Taiwan. She is the author of *Learning Nature* (2010), and *Education between Speech and Writing: Crossing the Boundaries of Dao and Deconstruction* (2017), as well as many philosophical and educational articles.

Hongde Lei is Associate Professor in the School of Education at Huazhong University of Science and Technology, Wuhan, China. His research focuses on institutional research, philosophy of philosophy, college teaching, and history of higher education.

Ren-Jie Vincent Lin has completed a PhD at the Institute of Education, University College London, UK. His research interests focus on histories of East–West cultural interactions, East Asia's modern learning from the West, and the transformation of Chinese government study-abroad scholarships.

Chunlei Lu is Professor in the Department of Teacher Education at Brock University, Canada, where he is also the Co-Director of the Confucius Institute. He has teaching experiences in seven universities in various countries. Based on these cross-cultural experiences, his research interests have concentrated on the overlapped areas of culture, education, and health.

Leonard Tan is Assistant Professor at the National Institute of Education, Nanyang Technological University, Singapore. His research interests include cross-cultural philosophical and empirical research in music education, and research on performing arts ensembles. He is the editor of *Empowering Student Voice: Developing the 21st Century Learner Musically* (with S.C. Leong, 2017).

Chia-Ling Wang is Associate Professor and Chair at the Institute of Education, National Taiwan Ocean University. Her research interests include philosophy of education, curriculum theories, and higher education. Her current research projects involve explorations of ecological philosophy in educational theories.

Hektor K.T. Yan is Assistant Professor in the Department of Public Policy, City University of Hong Kong, where he teaches Philosophy and Ethics. His recent publications include 'Epicurus, death and grammar' (*Philosophia*, 2014), and 'On experimental philosophy, morality and meaning' (*Philosophy*, 2016).

INTRODUCTION
Kaleidoscopic View of Chinese Philosophy of Education

In an article published in *The Guardian* on 9 April 2016, Michael Puett and Christine Gross-Loh—the authors of *The Path: What Chinese Philosophers Can Teach Us About the Good Life*—pose the question of why the history of Chinese philosophy is the currently most popular course at Harvard? As Puett and Gross-Loh describe, the ancient Chinese thinkers were neither rigid traditionalists nor placid preachers. Rather, they were exciting and radical thinkers, different from the Western thinkers: Western thinkers prefer to pose 'big' questions such as what and who we are, whereas Chinese thinkers like to ask 'small' and pragmatic questions that start from the mundane and doable. In this article, Puett and Gross-Loh pointed out several interesting 'alternative' ideas offered by Chinese thinkers. They include 'Stop finding yourself', 'Be inauthentic', 'Do rituals', 'See the world as capricious', 'Stop deciding', 'Be weak', 'Don't play to your strengths', 'Don't be mindful' and 'Rethink the tradition and the modern'.

Of course, each of these ideas is worth much discussion beyond the pursuit of this issue. However, hidden behind the ideas is a presupposed dichotomy between the Western and Chinese thoughts in spite of the fact that Chinese philosophy, in contrast to the Western philosophy, is thought by many authors to be strongly attentive to the issues of cultivation of the self, the social order or the harmony between human beings and nature (Ivanhoe, 2000; Tu, 1978), or, as Puett and Gross-Loh suggest, to the ideas alternative to the Western ones. It is indeed a hopeful anticipation to solely extract the key to the solution to the difficulty of life or the path towards utopia from the teachings of ancient Chinese wisdom. The concept of Chinese philosophy or Chinese culture is indeed vague and unclear. Confucianism is usually seen to represent traditional Chinese philosophy—'an integral part of East Asia and so salient a feature of the Sinic world' (Tu, 2000). However, this opinion seems to ignore other schools of thought such as Daoism and Buddhism. When Confucianism is taken as the main reference, we get to know that the geographical areas influenced by Confucianism include China, Japan, Korea, Taiwan, Hong Kong and Vietnam; these societies are termed as Confucian heritage cultures (CHC). The concept of CHC runs the risk of reducing or confusing the differences among these societies in the aspect of language, religion and history. Furthermore, if Chinese philosophy indicates a China-born philosophy, Buddhism has its roots in the religious thought of ancient

India. In what sense is Buddhism considered as an element of Chinese philosophy? The more attempts that we make to define the domain of Chinese philosophy, the more ambiguities we encounter. Ideas evolve all the time. It has always been a challenge to draw clear boundaries between schools of thought and define Chinese philosophy of education. Especially, in modern times, educational practices are influenced by the diverse and miscellaneous relevance of the global village where rapidly exchange and interaction is occurring in all aspects of life. Is Chinese philosophy of education the Chinese way of philosophising education? Is there a particular Chinese way of philosophising? As philosophising is usually understood as exercising the mind to seek the truth and knowledge, where does the particularity of Chinese philosophy fit in? Is it a particular way of exercising the mind to seek the truth and knowledge or a particular truth and knowledge? However, as exercising the mind is an intellectual activity, it seems to be more rational to suggest that the particularity of Chinese philosophy of education lies in the subject matter to be philosophised. Thus, Chinese philosophy of education could broadly include philosophical discussion and reflection of education based on Chinese thoughts but with considerations of the influence of the West or with the interaction between Chinese and non-Chinese cultures. In this vein, comparative studies provide many inspirations. With the increase in studies of comparative philosophy, we have seen increasingly fascinating and exciting similarities or resonances between Chinese and the Western thoughts (Burik, 2010; Hung, 2015; Li, 1999). Without daring to claim the scope of Chinese philosophy of education, this special issue is intended to let the heteroglossia concerning Chinese philosophy of education be heard, by giving space to diverse considerations of various themes. The themes include the genealogy of the Westernisation of Chinese education, cultivation of the self with respect to deep ecology, Daoism and Buddhism, Daoist mindful education from the perspective of postmodernism, contemporary interpretation of Confucian pedagogy and Chinese identity from the lens of criticality.

The first article, written by Ren-Jie Lin, traces back the history of the Westernisation or modernisation of education of China in the late Qing Dynasty (1616–1912) with particular focus on the contribution of overseas students with governmental sponsorship in the early twentieth century. Western contact with China dates back to mediaeval times, around the second-half of the thirteenth century. China was ruled by the Mongol Empire, the strength and prosperity of which impressed Europeans deeply. However, the rulers of the succeeding dynasties of imperial China also showed great pride and confidence when facing the West, until the First Opium War in 1839–1842. The loss of the Opium Wars and other conflicts with foreign countries forced the Chinese government and intellectuals of the late Qing Dynasty to initiate the movement of Westernisation (西化運動), to learn from the West. This was a process full of struggles and conflicts. Chinese intellectuals were proud and valued their own culture. To learn from the West, implying the recognition of self-deficiency, shattered the national pride and esteem. There was an idea formulated among Chinese intellectuals that became the principle of the movement. The principle of absorbing the Western advantages without losing identity was formulated into the motto: 'Zhong Ti Xi Yong' (中體西用), literally meaning 'Chinese learning for fundamentals while Western learning for practical application'. The viability of the very interesting concept of 'Zhong Ti Xi Yong' is surely worth more discussion; however, Lin does not spend much time on this concept. His aim is to introduce how the Qing Dynasty implemented the policy; sending students overseas was one of the schemes, who were helpful in greatly influencing modern China in many aspects. Lin's paper sketches the contour of the Westernisation of modern Chinese education.

Hektor Yan's article *Learning from the Barbarians? Reflections on Chinese Identity and 'Race' in the Educational Context* provides a novel and critical lens for the understanding of the notion of identity with respect to traditional Chinese culture and modern curriculum in Hong Kong. There has been a strong and age-old nationalism embedded in Chinese history and culture, which asserts that Chinese people are a nation distinguished from all other nations around—the so-called 'differentiation between Huá and Yí' (華夷之辨) or 'differentiation between Yí and Xià' (夷夏之辨), meaning 'the differentiation between Chinese and barbarians'. Yí generally means all tribal people but Chinese, whereas Huá or Xià means Chinese people only. Terms of this kind can be found in many ancient Confucian classics such as *the Analects* and *Liji, Xunzi* (Wu, 2013). As described in these classics, Chinese people strongly claimed the excellence in their own culture and civilisation as distinct from that of other tribes. And they still do in some sense. As the national self-confidence can be found in the ancient literature, it is extremely interesting to read the story about King Wuling of Zhào (325–299 BCE), who reigned in the State of Zhào during the Warring States period of Chinese history. The Warring States period is the second-half of the Eastern Zhou Dynasty when the ruling power of King of Zhou Dynasty was weak and the dukes of states proclaimed themselves as kings. King Wuling was one of the self-proclaiming kings; to strengthen the military power, he conducted reforms of 'Barbarian costumes and horseback archery' (胡服騎射), which initiated debates and criticisms. From the historical debates, Yan aptly reveals the age-old issue concerning national identity and its educational implications for modern Hong Kong. The story of King Wuling provides a lens for critically examining the notion of national identity taught in contemporary educational practice, e.g. using textbooks. In recent years, the issues about citizenship education and nationalistic education have aroused a lot of discussions (Lee, 2004; Leung & Print, 2002). In order to build and to strengthen the Chinese solidarity as well as identity among Hong Kong people, the concept of 'race' plays an important role. As Yan states, the concept of Chinese race is taught as natural and inbred. The point is that this conceptualisation is not new. It can date back to the past—from the debates aroused by the reforms of 'Barbarian costumes and horseback archery' in the Warring States period of time. More interesting is the fact that King Wuling convinced his people to take the reforms and thereby strengthened the military power of the kingdom in few years. The historical narrative, as Yan notes, calls for deep reflection upon the meaning of 'race' and 'identity', which should not be taken as natural and essential as they are conventionally understood in the traditional literature.

The following two articles both relate to the modern interpretation and contextualisation of Confucian pedagogy and pedagogue—the word 'pedagogue' is not used in its Greek origin to refer to a teacher slave, but only 'a teacher'. Leonard Tan's article *Confucius: Philosopher of Twenty-First Century Skills* aims to argue that the Confucian philosophy has great potential for implementing and improving the learning innovative skills required in the twenty-first century. As Tan notes, the key learning innovative skills, including critical thinking, communication and collaboration and creativity, have rich sources in the Confucian philosophy. This does not mean that the twenty-first-century learning skills are already contained in the ancient texts but that the Confucian wisdom provides rich sources for understanding these skills and contextualising them in the Confucian societies.

Hong-de Lei's *Problem-centred Design and Personal Teaching Style: An Exploratory Study of Youguang Tu's Course on Philosophy of Education* provides readers with a genuine story of Confucian pedagogue. Lei introduces readers—most of whom are unfamiliar with the ideas and practices of philosophy of education in contemporary China—to a pedagogical story about a contemporary Chinese philosopher of education, Youguang Tu (1927–2012). Tu underwent many turbulent and unsettling experiences in modern Chinese history in his whole life. He was respected as the most outstanding student of the contemporary prestigious philosopher Youlan Feng (1895–1990). Through the Cultural Revolution, Tu stood fast as a loyal scholar at restoring Feng's philosophy and as a diligent teacher of the philosophy of education. As Lei writes, Tu has a far-reaching influence upon academia. This paper thus widens the horizon of philosophy of education of contemporary China for readers outside China in the light of Tu's ideas and modes of teaching.

The following two papers do not deal with the most prominent theme—Confucianism—in the field of Chinese philosophy. Chia-Ling Wang's article is titled *Toward Self-Realisation: Exploring the ecological Self for education*. This paper argues for the concept of ecological self based on Norwegian philosopher Arne Naess' deep ecology, Buddhist and Daoist teachings. Wang argues that an in-depth understanding of the ecological self can be achieved from the perspectives of Naess', Buddhist and Daoist philosophies, all of which contribute to the formation of holistic view and the unity of humans and nature. Education with a holistic inspiration tends to encourage students to pay more attention to the non-human world, or in Abram's (1997) terms, the more-than-human world and thereby to widen the understanding of the self beyond the limits of egotism.

The next article is *Contextualising Postmodernity in Daoist Symbolism: Toward a Mindful Education Embracing Eastern Wisdom* written by Rob Blom and Chunlei Lu. Like Wang's article, this pays attention to education in the holistic and ecological context. The authors point out that there has been a prevalent belief concerning the worldview that is situated between the opposition between modernism and postmodernism. From the lens of the belief, modernist worldview defines the modes of thinking as rational, analytic, reductionist and linear. It also gives preferences to competitive and quantitative value systems. However, in the camp of postmodern worldview are modes of thinking with the characteristics of being intuitive, synthetic, holistic and non-linear and values of cooperation and equality. As the authors claim, the modern worldview can be labelled as 'masculine' (yáng), whereas the postmodern worldview is 'feminine' (ying) in the terms of Daoism. To elaborate the contrast between these two modes of thought, Blom and Lu consider issues with respect to various themes such as environmental problems, the concept of nature, system theory and the body–mind dualism. As the authors argue, the oppositional scheme of thinking modernism and postmodernism is a certain reductionist metaphysical mode of thought that may result in many theoretical and practical problems, including the compartmentalisation of education, agriculture and science. The authors attempt to propose an alternative—or holistic—framework with the inspiration of Daoist integral and dynamical concepts of yīng and yáng to give a more mindful approach to the understanding of the world. Based on the above, Blom and Lu suggest a mindful education that is able to embrace the eastern wisdom that would help in understanding the world in an inclusive way and to provide a careful treatment of education. For me, Chia-Ling Wang's and Rob Blom and Chunlei Lu's papers both suggest that the holistic metaphysical view implied in Chinese philosophy contributes to build an environmentally friendly education. Nevertheless, what is noteworthy is that their papers lack criticality towards the sociopolitical–socio-economic structures in relation to ecological problems.

Translation, the Knowledge Economy, and Crossing Boundaries in Contemporary Education written by Viola Y. Chen discusses about the interplay between knowledge, translation and culturally creative economy in the context of global education. Translation plays a tricky role in the contemporary global world. Does translation improve communication between societies of different cultures and languages? Or does it result in misunderstanding? Chen focuses on the role of translation in educational settings when creative knowledge and knowledge economy crossing borders of cultures, languages, states and traditions are in need. The so-called good translation needs be achieved based on 'correct understanding, precise interpretation and representation of different cultures s through various languages'. It is not only about the enhancement of second-language ability, but involves the wide and broad understanding of different cultures and societies with respect to history and politics. After reading this article, I dare not say that education of translation and interpretation aims to produce 'correct' translation. Perhaps a better way of describing the education of translation is that it prepares students to be more flexible and open to the new world. Then the crossing of boundaries is possible.

The articles included in this issue provide a variety of, but not exclusive, ways of conceptualising Chinese philosophy of education in the postmodern times. I do not have a clear and definite answer to the scope, limits, questions, subject matter and paradigm of Chinese philosophy of education. In the miscellaneous world or worlds, this special issue lends a kaleidoscope for viewers to see parts of the features of Chinese philosophy of education that survives and evolves shifting time and space.

References

Abram, D. (1997). *The spell of the sensuous: Perception and language in a more-than-human world.* New York, NY: Vintage.
Burik, S. (2010). *End of comparative philosophy and the task of comparative thinking: Heidegger, Derrida, and Daoism.* Albany, NY: SUNY Press.
Hung, R. (2015). To be *as* not to be: In search of an alternative humanism in the light of early Daoism and deconstruction. *Journal of Philosophy of Education, 49,* 418–434.
Ivanhoe, P. J. (2000). *Confucian moral self cultivation.* Indianapolis, IN: Hackett Publishing.

Lee, W. O. (2004). Citizenship education in Hong Kong: Development and challenges. In W. O., Lee, D. L., Grossman, K. J., Kennedy, & G. P., Fairbrother (Eds.) *Citizenship education in Asia and the Pacific: Concepts and issues* (pp. 59–80). New York, NY: Kluwer Academic Publisher.

Leung, Y. W., & Print, M. (2002). Nationalistic education as the focus for civics and citizenship education: The case of Hong Kong. *Asia Pacific Education Review, 3*, 197–209.

Li, C. (1999). *The Tao encounters the west: Explorations in comparative philosophy*. Albany, NY: SUNY Press.

Puett, M., & Gross-Loh, C. (2016, April 9). Forget mindfulness, stop trying to find yourself and start faking it. *The Guardian*. Retrieved from https://www.theguardian.com/books/2016/apr/09/forget-mindfulness-stop-trying-to-find-yourself-start-faking-it-confucius

Tu, W. (1978). *Humanity and self-cultivation: Essays in Confucian thought*. Boston, MA: Cheng & Tsui.

Tu, W. (2000). Implications of the rise of "Confucian" East Asia. *Daedalus, 129*, 195–218.

Wu, X.-M. (2013). Between different cultures: Identification, differentiation, and exchange. *Taiwan Journal of East Asian Studies, 10*, 273–298. (Chinese). doi: 10.6163/tjeas.2013.10(2)273

RUYU HUNG

Eastward Expansion of Western Learning: A study of Westernisation of China's modern education by Chinese government overseas-study scholarships

REN-JIE VINCENT LIN

Abstract

This article aims to trace back the history of how Chinese Government attempted to strengthen its national power by learning from the USA, Western Europe and Japan since the mid-nineteenth century, as well as to analyse the influences Westernisation had on the development of China's modern education. In this process, the Chinese Government overseas-study scholarships played a key role in speeding up China's learning from the West, and assisted numerous students in experiencing Western modernisation while they studied abroad. By examining this historical retrospect, some findings are concluded from this research. First, several significant conflicts between China and foreign countries stimulated Chinese officials deeply to learn the knowledge and skills of Western navy, military, sciences, technologies and philosophies. Second, Chinese scholars also began to reflect and criticise the influence of these Westernised reforms on Chinese traditional culture and values.

Background: Histories of China-West interactions

Interactions between China and the West in culture, religion, technology and consumption products had been expanded by Chinese and European traders, Catholic and Christian missionaries, Buddhist monks, travellers and Islamic merchants before the sixteenth century (Chen, 2002). Since the sixteenth century, printing was invented and improved in China and the West, so knowledge and technologies could be largely and intermediately dispersed (Burke, 2012). This mutual influence in disseminating knowledge was greatly expanded and distributed more broadly across national borders and geographical boundaries.

For example, Islamic traders and scholars, such as Martino Martini, the Italian Catholic Sinologist, and Jacob Golius, the Dutch Protestant Arabist, can be seen as transmitters of knowledge diffused between China and the West (Burke, 2000). Originally encountered in Leiden in 1654, Martino translated the history of transnational knowledge distribution recorded in Chinese documents into Latin, and Golius simultaneously translated Arabic documents into Latin. Therefore, this connected history of cultural interactions can be found in some historical documents.

In addition to these traders, Catholic missionaries also played an important role in promoting the transmission of knowledge between China and the West. For example, Matteo Ricci, the Italian Jesuit missionary, not only introduced the achievements of European science, mathematics and philosophy to China, which stimulated Chinese scholars and officials to learn Western academic knowledge, but also introduced the Confucian classics to Europe and translated them into Latin. In addition, the German scholar, Athanasius Kircher, and the French scholar Jean-Baptiste du Halde also recorded the Chinese experiences of Martino Martini, Michael Boyd and other missionaries. This contributed to the rise of a certain 'Sinology fever' in Western Europe from the mid-seventeenth century to the eighteenth century (Yan, 2002).

However, China, as well as Japan, had implemented an isolationist policy from the late seventeenth century, during which time, the West experienced industrial and scientific revolutions, which propelled Western countries to become more modernised. Then, the West's increasingly hostile attitude towards China and Japan in the mid-nineteenth century forced the Chinese and Japanese governments to renew their contacts with the West.

From the late nineteenth century, after a policy of diplomatic isolation that lasted for several hundred years and following military defeats by Western powers, the Chinese Government was eventually persuaded by some Chinese intellectuals to expand its Western learning journey. In order to acquire the latest technologies from the West, official scholarships were established by Chinese central and provincial governments to send students to study in the USA, Western Europe and Japan from 1872.

Having experienced defeat in several wars with the West and in order to build a new modern education system, the Chinese Government and scholars at the time planned to borrow and learn from Western countries' experience (T.-C. Liu, 2005). Therefore, from the late nineteenth century, the process of disseminating knowledge can be found to have been transformed from one of mutual exchange to one of single learning means.

For a long period, China's contemporary learning journey was mainly influenced by the USA, Western Europe and Japan. Chou (2014) and Wang (2013) have examined the academic interactions between modern Japan and China. Liou (2007a, 2007b, 2008) has analysed the process of how German pedagogy was introduced and transferred into wartime China. Most importantly, the USA has always played a significant role on the development of China's modernisation since the twentieth century, as was stressed by Li (2000) and Liou (2013). As to the topic of the Eastward expansion of Western learning, Wu (2005, 2009) and Chen (2008) have pointed out how Western modern thought was disseminated through wartime China and how Chinese intellectuals dealt with Western challenges to Chinese traditional culture.

Regarding the contributions of Chinese students overseas to the academic interactions between China and the West, Li (1987, 2005, 2006, 2010) has published numerous studies, examining how these Chinese students' study-abroad experience introduced Western knowledge and technologies to China and helped the Chinese Government to improve its nation's power. Following Li's studies, X.-Q. Liu (2005) focused on how Chinese students in Britain played significant roles in the process of China's modernisation reforms by analysing the Chinese Government's policies of overseas education.

Centred on the Chinese nineteenth-century context, this research aims to examine the history of China's modern scholarly interaction with the USA, Western Europe and Japan, with special reference to Chinese intellectuals' contributions to expand the Westernised movement of China's modern educational system. Why and how China would like to learn from the West and Japan? Subsequently, the official study-abroad scholarship founded by Chinese Government, which assisted Chinese scholars to undertake their overseas studies and to disseminate Western modern thoughts and sciences in China, is a key factor. It means why the Chinese would like to found the overseas-study scholarship at that time and what contributions were supported by these Chinese overseas-study scholarship receivers? Finally, when Western knowledge was received in China, Chinese intellectuals began to debate the influence of these Westernised reforms on Chinese traditional culture and values. In other words, how Chinese intellectuals faced the dilemma between Chinese traditional culture and Western modernisation. This will be dealt with in the third section of this article.

China's and Japan's Modern Journey of Learning from the West

The academic exchange between China and Europe was initially processed by Western priests and traders in the sixteenth century. The Italian Jesuit priest, Matteo Ricci, who lived in China between 1583 and 1610, is usually regarded as being the first contributor among these culture mediators. During his stay in China, he not only introduced the development of European science, mathematics and philosophy to China, which motivated Chinese scholars and officials to learn Western knowledge, but also simultaneously translated the Confucian classics into Latin, which encouraged Europeans to consider Chinese culture (Bernard, 1935; Fontana, 2011; Zhang, 2002). The cultural communication between China and Europe subsequently became a sort of 'cultural fever' in the seventeenth and early eighteenth centuries (Yan, 2002).

However, for many reasons, including the continual widespread conflict of religious cognition, the Qing Dynasty Government decided to implement a policy of isolationism from 1723. In fact, the Japanese Government had also implemented the same policy in Japan in 1633 for similar reasons. During this period, Western science and technology progressively advanced, while the Chinese and Japanese governments still refused to reopen the doors to their countries. In 1853, Japan was threatened by the US Navy, and was obliged to restart international trade with the United States, which stimulated the Japanese Government to reform and learn from the West from 1867. This was called the Meiji Restoration, when Japan witnessed the West's advanced technology and weapons. After the claim of *Departure from Asia* in 1885, the Japanese Government strictly monitored the progress of Westernisation (Nitobe, 1931).

Therefore, Japan is considered to have been the first modernised country in Asia because of its Westernised movement. During this period, Japanese scholars adapted Western knowledge in a massive scale and translated numerous Western publications, which were gradually introduced and translated into Chinese by Chinese scholars to reflect the development of the West.

In fact, Japanese culture originated in China and Japan was also deeply influenced by Confucianism. Therefore, when the Japanese Government and scholars transformed their learning to Western philosophies and civilisation, they also faced the problem of accommodating them (Nitobe, 1931; Yamasaki, 2010). In other words, learning to think and behave like Westerners became an important task for the Japanese at that time.

Although more and more Japanese scholars have reflected on the influence of Westernisation and Americanisation currents on the development of educational studies in Japan for the past several decades (Horio, 1988; Inatomi, 1973; Yoshida, 1931), Western educational studies are still highly regarded and borrowed by the Japanese educational academic community, as well as Chinese educationalists.

In China, the Qing Dynasty Government decided to learn from the West after experiencing defeat in two wars, namely, the Opium War against the Victorian United Kingdom (UK) in 1840 and the Sino-Japanese War in 1894–1895. At that time, the main interest of the Chinese Government and scholars was Western technology and military force rather than Western educational knowledge (Chung, 2000; Fairbank, 1978; Fairbank & Liu, 1980; Hillemann, 2009). In terms of the current research, only five of the foreign scholarly books translated and introduced to China by European priests before 1895 were related to European education systems and ideas, including the British educationalist, Herbert Spencer's *What Knowledge is of Most Worth*, which was translated into Chinese in 1882, whereas the subjects of most other books appeared to be Western science and technology (Zhou, 1996).

From 1897, the Qing Dynasty attempted to establish a modern schooling system in China, a teacher education system and a study of education by borrowing experiences from the West (Ayers, 1971; T.-C. Liu, 2005). At that time, the dominant foreign educational knowledge disseminated in China came from the USA and Germany (Wu, 2005). Figure 1 illustrates that there were two main routes for China to learn from the West before and after the 1920s.

In the beginning, based on the fact that Japan had succeeded in learning from the West since 1867 and numerous Western books had been translated into Japanese, the Chinese Government and scholars regarded Japan as being a successful westernised example and considered that learning from Japan would be the approach that would bring them faster results (Wei, 1998; Xiao, 2002).

Therefore, the books that had been translated into Japanese were retranslated into Chinese, published as books and journal articles. In addition, from a geographical perspective, since Japan is closer to China than the USA or Europe, the Chinese

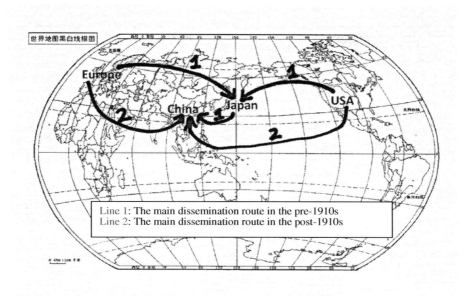

Figure 1: The main routes of the dissemination of Western knowledge into China pre- and post-1910 (Lin, 2014, p. 81).

Government could send numerous Chinese students to Japan to learn Western knowledge on a lower budget. Language was another factor to consider. Unlike the alphabet used in English, French, German or Italian, Japanese characters were originally based on Chinese characters. So, Japanese was arguably the easiest of all foreign languages for Chinese students to learn and understand. Lastly, China and Japan had a similar culture, and simultaneously faced the tide of Western culture and force.

However, Japan had been westernised earlier than China, and the Japanese had selected the Western advanced knowledge they needed. Therefore, Chinese scholars believed that they could save much time by learning what they needed from Japan rather than directly from the West (Chou, 2011; Zhou, 1996). In other words, the Chinese Government and scholars believed that the knowledge Japan had selected from the West would also be what China needed, as illustrated by Figure 1.

It was inevitable that some problems would arise when the Chinese tried to understand the Western culture only from Japanese translations. Firstly, Western books were translated into Japanese and then translated again from Japanese into Chinese and the content of the Chinese translated version may not have completely equalled what the original author had intended to express. Secondly, during the process of translation, some translators may have deliberately selected only the information they needed or provided their own explanations of the content of the translated books to use in China, content that had never been written by the original Western authors (Liou, 2007b).

Academic and knowledge contacts and exchanges between modern China and the West developed in a broadly similar way to the relationship of knowledge dissemination in China and the West before the Sino-Japanese War of 1895, are analysed in Figure 1. From the 1910s, increasing numbers of students under government scholarships finished their PhD in the USA and other Western countries and went back to China. Therefore, Western academic educational knowledge could be gradually understood directly by Chinese scholars, without further reliance on translation from the Japanese language.

A Critical Reflection on 'Xi Xue Dong Jian' and 'Zhong Ti Xi Yong'

During the learning process for China, the two terms are always very important while controversial. The first term of 'Xi Xue Dong Jian' means the process of Eastward expansion of Western learning and the second term of 'Zhong Ti Xi Yong' means Chinese learning for fundamentals while Western learning for practical application. For the former term of 'Xi Xue Dong Jian', the representative of the classic novels, *Fortress Besieged*, written by Zhongshu Qian indeed reflected Chinese intellectuals' dilemma between these two cultures. For the latter term, many academic debates on the topic of 'Zhong Ti Xi Yong' were once raised by Chinese intellectuals who supported 'Zhong Xue' (Chinese culture), 'Xi Xue' (Western culture) or the mix of 'Zhong Xue' and 'Xi Xue' to argue which one was better for China at that time (Ayers, 1971; Bays, 1978; Eastman, 1968). The similar and significant debates also happened in the field of educational philosophy in China between 1920s and 1930s (Wu, 2005). From 'Xi Xue Dong Jian' to 'Zhong Ti Xi Yong', it can be found that Confucianism was challenged drastically by Western philosophies, technologies and sciences (Levenson, 1965; Wright, 1957).

Wars, Chinese Overseas Education and Chinese Government Study-Abroad Scholarships

In terms of the process of learning from the West in pre-1949 China, Chinese Government study-abroad scholarships played an important role in encouraging Chinese intellectuals to expand the number of scholarly exchanges and borrow Western academic contributions and experiences. However, one of the main factors to stimulate the Chinese Government to learn from the West, to open its overseas education and to establish the official study-abroad scholarships was that China experienced three significant wars, including the Opium War in 1842, the Sino-Japanese War in 1895 and the Eight-Nation Alliance War in 1900.

By examining the history of Chinese students' overseas study in the UK, Kuan Huang (1829–1878) can be regarded as the first Chinese to study in the UK. Supported by American and British traders, Huang studied at the University of Edinburg, in Scotland, between 1850 and 1855, and then undertook an internship for 2 years. In 1857, Huang concluded his PhD in medicine. After returning to China, Huang also disseminated into China the advanced knowledge of Western medicine he had gained abroad (X.-Q. Liu, 2005). However, Huang's contributions could not persuade the Chinese Government to set more scholarships for students to study in the UK.

In fact, after being defeated by the UK in the Opium War, in 1842, the Chinese Government understood the importance of developing the country's navy. However, due to issues of national self-esteem and conflicts of inward–outward oscillation, the Chinese Government did not expand policies of overseas education. In 1877, Chinese officials finally began to establish scholarships to send the first Chinese students to study at The Royal Naval College Greenwich, including the famous translator Fu Yan. During this period, some Chinese students also began to study science and technology in Britain. However, this policy was soon suspended because most Chinese officials were excessively conservative and bureaucratic and were unable to concede that China should learn from the West. It can be concluded that the Opium War reopened Chinese officials' minds to the need to foster contact with the West but this was not enough to transform these ideas into practical policies and actions.

Compared to China–Britain interactions, the academic relation between China and the USA had started earlier. Actually, the history of the government study-abroad scholarships can be retraced to 1872 when 30 Chinese children were sent to study in USA by the Chinese Government, as recommended and advocated by Wing Yung (Chu, 1977; Shu, 1989). Yung came from Guangdong Province and became one of the first study-abroad students in modern China with the support of American missionaries (LaFargue, 1987). After obtaining his Bachelor of Arts at Yale University in 1854, he returned to China in 1855. Having observed his motherland being weak and invaded for a long time, Yung realised the importance of establishing government scholarships for Chinese students to study in Western countries to acquire new knowledge. Subsequently, he successfully persuaded the central government and provincial authorities to fund official scholarships for Chinese students to study in the USA from 1872, in Europe from 1877 and in Japan from 1897 (Cheng, 2003; Chiang, 1934; Lin, 1994). However, due to the pressure of more conservative Chinese officials, as mentioned above, the Chinese students studying in the USA were requested to suspend their studies and to return to China.

According to a number of sources, a total of 2000 Chinese students was studying in USA in 1920, while the UK only attracted 270 (Cheng, 2003; Shu, 1926). In addition to the USA and Britain, the most popular country for Chinese students to study during this period was Japan. A number of factors can explain why the Chinese Government still preferred to send students to in Japan rather than the USA and Britain (Chou, 2011; Zhou, 1996). Firstly, Japan is geographically close to China, which meant sponsorship would require a smaller budget as well as make it easier to monitor these students' performance. Secondly, China and Japan have a similar culture. In fact, the Japanese culture came from China, and is also deeply influenced by Confucianism, which enabled Chinese students to overcome some cultural differences. Thirdly, the Japanese language is formed by Chinese characters, so it was easier for Chinese students to learn Japanese rather than other foreign languages. Fourthly, the Westernised movement of the Meiji Restoration contributed to making Japan into a modern country, which also inspired the Chinese Government to borrow successful experiences from its neighbour.

According to official records, the Chinese Government sent most Chinese students to study in Japan before the twentieth century, rather than in other foreign countries. Numerous female students were sent to Japan for normal education in the hope that they would acquire new knowledge and become primary and high school teachers in China's new education system, which was established in the early twentieth century (Shu, 1926). In 1895, the Sino-Japanese War broke out, and Japan's victory stimulated the Chinese Government to set scholarships to send more students to Japan (Cyu, 1975). However, in the 1910s, a Republican revolution occurred in China, causing the Chinese central and local governments' difficulties in affording the large budget for the study-abroad scholarships. Meanwhile, in 1908, the USA Government had decided to return the indemnity from the Eight-Nation Alliance War for the Chinese Government to set the Tsinghua Scholarship of study in the USA. Thirdly, the Japanese Government's desire to invade China stimulated Chinese students to reject studying in Japan. Therefore, Japan gradually lost its advantages for Chinese students from the 1910s onwards (Cyu, 1975; X.-Q. Liu, 2005; Shu, 1989).

The Sino-Japanese War stimulated academic relations between China and Japan, reflected in the fact that the Chinese Government decided to support scholarships for students to study in Japan, and stimulated Chinese officials to recognise the factors that could explain how Japan moved to modernisation since the Meiji Restoration. This is the reason why most of Chinese overseas students left for Japan rather than the USA and Western Europe before the 1910s.

Table 1 shows the distribution of Chinese students who acquired official scholarships to study overseas between 1921 and 1925. Although the official documents suffer from poor preservation and organisation, it can be concluded that most of the 1075 Chinese students studying in Japan had to pay their own fees and only a few were awarded government scholarships. The total number of Chinese Government scholarships awarded overall is not clear from these government archives.

At first, the main purpose of providing Chinese Government scholarships was to allow Chinese students to learn advanced Western military knowledge and technology in order to promote the development of China's national defence. For example, the first students sent to Britain in 1877 by the Chinese Government only studied expert naval knowledge and technology (X.-Q. Liu, 2005). As previously mentioned, recipients of the government scholarships were gradually permitted to study other fields, and the most popular subjects included engineering, business, medicine, law and agriculture (Shu, 1926). Besides, it should be noted that only a few Chinese students went abroad to learn the subject of educational studies, especially to Japan and the

Table 1: The distribution of countries chosen by Chinese students who acquired an official scholarship to study overseas, 1921–1925 (Shu, 1926, pp. 229–230).

	Country chosen by Chinese students						
	Japan	USA	Germany	France	Britain	others	Total
Number	1075	934	127	89	29	328	2582
Percentage	41.51%	33.85%	4.92%	3.45%	1.12%	12.70%	100%

USA, and the majority of those were women studying normal education (Shu, 1926). This demonstrates that schooling in China needed the stimulation of Western educational knowledge at that time and there was a deeply rooted opinion that teaching should only be done by women.

The government's scholarship policy promoted the expansion of more successful academic exchanges between China and foreign countries in wartime. It also made a significant contribution to recipients who were studying arts and humanities, since unlike postgraduates who wanted to study science, who had more chances of being awarded a foreign scholarship to study overseas, most Chinese arts and humanities researchers, such as those in the field of educational studies, usually had to rely on a government scholarship to study abroad (Chen, 2013).

The third outward war here considered is the Eight-Nation Alliance War, which eventually pushed the Chinese Government to support more Chinese students to leave for the USA. In order to reopen China's trade market, which was tightly controlled by the Qing Dynasty's isolationist policy in the nineteenth century, Western countries started to expand into China, what generated a number of conflicts. After the Opium War in 1842, the Chinese Government experienced several military defeats, and it was obligated to pay indemnities to the invaders. Having experienced massive defeat in war and invasion by foreign countries, the policy of study-abroad scholarships was again implemented by the Chinese in the twentieth century.

In 1900, the war caused by the Boxer Rebellion ended with China's defeat by the Eight-Nation Alliance of Italy, USA, France, Austria-Hungary, Japan, Germany, the UK and Russia. According to the Boxer protocol, the Chinese Government had to pay a costly indemnity to these eight countries. In 1908, the United States Congress decided to return most of the indemnity to China and asked the Chinese Government to manage this indemnity to set an overseas scholarship for Chinese students to study in the USA. This scholarship was named the Boxer Indemnity Scholarship or the Tsinghua Scholarship (Shu, 1926). This policy made by the USA also increased the numbers of Chinese students studying in USA, and the US gradually surpassed Japan to become the country which received the largest number of Chinese overseas students from the 1910s.

Following the American Government's policy to attract more Chinese students and strengthen academic interactions, in 1926, the British Parliament and British intellectuals, such as B. Russell, also promoted plans to follow the American Government's strategy to invest this indemnity on overseas study for Chinese students. According to official documents, a total of 193 Chinese students were selected and sent to study in the UK from 1933 to 1946 (X.-Q. Liu, 2005). After finishing their studies and returning to China, these Chinese students made significant contributions to China's modernisation. With the change of political regimes in post-1949 China, the Sino-British Boxer Indemnity Scholarship was eventually suspended.

The number of Chinese students leaving for the USA surpassed those leaving for Japan since the 1910s, owing to the Tsinghua Scholarship. Therefore, the Eight-Alliance Nation War was a watershed for Chinese overseas education. During the Second World War, China was, with the USA, part of the Allies, fighting together to defeat Japan, which was another decisive factor to encourage more and more Chinese students to study in the USA rather than other countries.

In conclusion, these three significant wars expanded the Chinese Government overseas education policy. The Opium War in 1842 awakened the Chinese Government to gain consciousness of the weakness of the nation. After several decades, the Chinese Government eventually planned to send its students abroad to learn naval knowledge, sciences and technology since 1872. However, the Sino-Japanese War in 1895 evidenced the failure of the Chinese Government's Western learning strategy, focusing on technologies and sciences rather than humanities and social sciences, and stressing the skills and the applications rather than fundamental and spiritual thoughts. The Sino-Japanese War forced China to face its neighbour and experience Japan's rebirth after the Meiji Restoration. It is undoubtedly true that this war promoted more academic interactions between China and Japan, and that the Chinese Government made good use of these official scholarships to support more students to study in Japan until the 1910s. Before this war, Chinese intellectuals began to reflect and criticise how to find a balance between keeping Chinese traditional ideas, values and heritage and learning Western advanced technologies, skills and science. After this war, another question gradually appeared that learning from the West should be focused on the material or the spiritual level.

Finally, after the Eight-Nation Alliance War in 1900 and the establishment of the Tsinghua Scholarship in 1908, the USA gradually replaced Japan as Chinese students' favourite destination for their overseas studies, and this trend grew stably since the 1910s.

Chinese Official Study-Abroad Scholarship Receivers' Contributions to Westernisation of China's Modern Education System

With the influence of Eastward expansion of Western learning in China since the latter half of the nineteenth century, the demands of the Westernised movement of the education reform also challenged the Chinese traditional educational system. In 1898, the *Act to Constitute the Imperial University* requested a more systematic organisation of Western-style universities where Chinese classics and Western academic foundations could be combined. In 1902, the *Act to Constitute New Schools* called for more completely Western-style schools in China. However, this policy would not be carried out because of specific political factors. In 1904, the *Memorandum to Fix the Rules and Regulations for New Schools* became official policy, which claimed the complete Westernisation of all schools and the integration of Chinese classics into Western curriculum. As to China's *National Civil Servant Examination System*, it could not be abolished until 1905 (Wu, 2009).

On the evolution of implementing educational reforms, Chinese ambassadors, representatives and officials were often sent to Japan and other countries and then made substantial and practical suggestions to the Chinese Government based on their observations abroad. However, these foreign countries were taking frequent and speedy reforms at that time, so it would be difficult to keep pace with them. Therefore, it was questioned if this kind of short stays could actually help these Chinese officials to understand these foreign countries' specific contexts completely, such as Ju-Lun Wu's and Chen-Yu Lo's stays of several months for visiting Japanese educational reforms (Chou, 2014; Chung, 2000).

In addition to Chinese officials' overseas visits, Chinese students abroad also experienced the dramatic transformation of foreign countries' reforms by their observations in person for long periods of time. Animated by patriotic feelings, most of these Chinese overseas students were eager to offer advice to the Chinese Government about reforms, especially these recipients of official study-abroad scholarships.

For example, Fu Yan was not only a famous translator who introduced American and British modern political philosophy into China but was also an advocator for supporting the Chinese Government's overseas education policy. When Yan was sent to study at the Royal Greenwich Naval College, he witnessed the national power of Britain. Therefore, he positively established Western-style schools and assisted the official study-abroad scholarship students to go overseas.

In addition to the contributions of these Chinese official scholarship students to study in Britain, another official scholarship sent students to study in the USA. Figures such as Shih Hu, Meng-Lin Jiang, Ping-Wen Kuo and Xing-Zhi Tao also attempted to cooperate with the central and provincial governments to contribute to the modernisation and Westernisation of Chinese educational reforms at that time, including establishing experiment schools, expanding Western-style higher education and publishing academic journals to introduce Western thought.

With the wave of Eastward expansion of Western learning since the mid-nineteenth century, some of Chinese officials and scholars began to advocate the Westernisation of educational reforms. During the same period of Japan's Meiji Restoration in 1867, the Westernisation Movement in China expanded from 1862, and it ended in 1895, with China's defeat in the First Sino-Japanese War. Although this Westernisation Movement was commonly regarded as a failed reform, it became the foundation for the May Fourth Movement in 1919.

During the Westernisation Movement, Zhi-Dong Zhang supported the debatable motto *Chung Ti Shi Yong* (Hsueh, 2001; Wu, 2009), that aimed to guide China's modernisation programme by using Chinese learning for the essential principles, while Western learning for practical applications. Zhang was not only the governor of the Hubei Province at that time but also a significant educational reformer. He never studied abroad, but he experienced the importance of Westernised reforms. He built up new Western schools in Hubei Province during the Westernisation Movement and advanced the establishment of Western educational institutions in the early twentieth century (Wu, 2009).

This statement of *Chung Ti Shi Yong* claimed by Zhang actually attracted Chinese officials' and scholars' concerns and debates. Compared to these radical reformers, most Chinese intellectuals with study-abroad experiences recognised the importance and essentiality of Westernised educational reforms after witnessing the speedy development of Western countries. But they still could not ignore the deep influence of Chinese traditional culture and values, cultivated by Confucianism and religion. Therefore, questions such as what China should learn from the West, how to fuse Western philosophies, technologies and sciences into China's specific context and how to search for a balance between Chinese culture and learning from the West, became controversial topics at that time.

This Westernisation Movement stressed the application of Western technologies and skills, while the May Fourth Movement mainly focused on the borrowing and learning of Western modern philosophy and thought. Chinese traditional culture, such as Confucianism, was progressively more challenged by Chinese study-abroad intellectuals. These different strings were not reconciled appropriately then. However, with the speedy growth of East and Southeast Asian economies in recent years, it seems that the Sinology fever is returning to the mainstream.

Concluding Remarks

While the Qing Dynasty's stayed in isolation, the West was experiencing the Scientific and Industrial Revolutions. With the rise of imperialism, Chinese Government decided to learn from the West after experiencing invasion and military defeat. The Opium War against the Victorian UK opened China's Western learning journey.

Since 1872, Chinese Government implemented its overseas education policy to send the first Chinese students to the USA, Western Europe and Japan. Most of what these overseas Chinese students learned was Western technology and skills, and consequently, the Westernisation Movement from 1862 to 1895 eventually ended in defeat in the Sino-Japanese War. During this period of learning from the West, the idea of *Zhong Ti Xi Yong* supported by Zhi-Dong Zhang gradually attracted Chinese officials and intellectuals to reflect and criticise how to find a successful path for China to combine different cultural aspects.

Facing inward–outward oscillation, patriotic students under the Chinese Government study-abroad scholarship scheme positively contributed to Westernised educational reforms after they witnessed the national power of some Western countries. They established Western-style schools, expanded Westernisation in higher education, reformed Chinese traditional curriculum and published academic journals to introduce modern Western thoughts. However, after several great debates, the fusion of Chinese and Western cultures was still an unresolvable lesson for these Chinese overseas students and other intellectuals.

With the economic recession of the West and the stable growth of East and Southeast economies in recent years, it seems that a 'Sinology fever' is gradually becoming popular again. Wars and the economy changed China, as well as the world. However, these government study-abroad scholarship students are still playing an important role in promoting mutual understandings between different peoples and cultures.

In this article, it addresses the development of China's official study-abroad scholarship recipients' contributions to the Westernisation movement of China's modern education from the historical approach. However, it still leaves two unresolved lessons and questions for the further research. First, it should be analysed deeply whether the development of China's official study-abroad scholarship policies was effected by the West, with the significant influence of these China's official scholarship intellectuals in China's academic world and official government since the twentieth century.

Second, with the huge evolution of Westernisation of China's modern education system, Chinese scholars and intellectuals criticised the positive and negative influences of Westernisation on China's traditional education system, and subsequently several great debates were also argued in public.

Disclosure statement

No potential conflict of interest was reported by the author.

References

Ayers, W. (1971). *Chang Chih-Tung and educational reform in China*. Cambridge, MA: Harvard University Press.
Bays, D. H. (1978). *China enters the twentieth century*. Ann Arbor, MI: The University of Michigan Press.
Bernard, H. (1935). *Matteo Ricci's scientific contribution to China*. (E. C. Werner, Trans.). Shanghai: The North China Daily News.
Burke, P. (2000). *A social history of knowledge: From Gutenberg to Diderot*. Cambridge: Polity.
Burke, P. (2012). *A social history of knowledge: From the Encyclopédie to Wikipedia* (Vol. II). Cambridge: Polity.
Chen, S.-S. (2002). *5000 years' history of cultural exchanges between China and the outside world* (Vol. 1). Beijing: World Knowledge Press.
Chen, W.-F. (2008). The fusion of Eastern and Western cultures: The cases of Nakamura Keiu and Yan Fu. *Taiwan Journal of East Asian Studies, 5*, 61–111.
Chen, Y.-S. (2013). *Modernisation or cultural imperialism: A critical reading of Taiwan's national scholarship programme for overseas study*. New York, NY: Peter Lang.
Cheng, X. (2003). *The study on modern Chinese students studying abroad*. Hong Kong: Hong Kong Social Sciences.
Chiang, S.-K. (1934). *The education system in modern China*. Shanghai: The Commercial.
Chou, Y.-W. (2011). The study of education development in the Republic of China in the twentieth century. In The Society of Chinese Education (Ed.), *The retrospect of the development of educational studies in ROC for one hundred years* (pp. 257–300). Taipei: The Pro-Ed Publishing.
Chou, Y.-W. (2014). Zunxian Huang's contribution to the introduction of aspects of the Japanese education system and the establishment of Western-style education in late Qing China. *Bulletin of Educational Research, 60*, 77–114.
Chu, L.-H. (1977). The history of Chinese students studying abroad. In Chinese Society of Education (Ed.), *The development of Chinese education* (pp. 464–480). Taipei: Fu-Hsin.
Chung, S.-H. (2000). *Moving toward the world: A history of modern Chinese intellectuals' visits in the West*. Beijing: Zhonghua, 2000.
Cyu, L.-H. (1975). *A study of planning our country and the policy of overseas education*. Taipei: The National Planning Council.
Eastman, L. E. (1968). Political reformism in China before the Sino-Japanese War. *Journal of Asian Studies, 27*, 111–132.

Fairbank, J. K. (Ed.). (1978). *Late Ch'ing 1800–1911 (Part 1)*. Cambridge: Cambridge University Press.

Fairbank, J. K., & Liu, K.-C. (Eds.). (1980). *Late Ch'ing 1800–1911 (Part 2)*. Cambridge: Cambridge University Press.

Fontana, M. (2011). *Matteo Ricci: A Jesuit in the Ming court*. Plymouth: Rowman & Littlefield.

Hillemann, U. (2009). *Asian empire and British knowledge: China and the networks of British imperial expansion*. Basingstoke: Palgrave MacMillan.

Horio, T. (1988). *Educational thought and ideology in modern Japan: State authority and intellectual freedom*. (S. Platzer, Trans.). Tokyo: University of Tokyo.

Hsueh, H.-Y. (2001). *On Chung Ti Shi Yong in the late Qing Dynasty: Chinese government's statements on Westernisation theories*. Taipei: Daw-Shiang Publishing.

Inatomi, E. (1973). Japanese culture and its education. *New Era, 54*, 79–82.

LaFargue, T. (1987). *China's first hundred: Educational mission students in the United States, 1872–1881*. Pullman, WA: Washington State University.

Levenson, J. R. (1965). *Confucian China and its modern fate*. Los Angeles, CA: The University of California Press.

Li, X.-S. (1987). *Students study abroad in modern China*. Beijing: People Press.

Li, Y.-S. (2000). *John Dewey and modern Chinese education: Prospects for a new philosophy* (Unpublished doctoral thesis). Ohio State University, Columbus, OH.

Li, X.-S. (Ed.). (2005). *Students study abroad and Chinese and Western cultures*. Tianjin: Nankai University Press.

Li, X.-S. (2006). *Students study abroad in modern times and Chinese and Western cultures*. Tianjin: Tianjin Education Press.

Li, X.-S. (2010). *The history of Chinese overseas education*. Guangdong: Guangdong Education Publishing House.

Lin, C.-F. (1994). *A documentary collection on Chinese students studying abroad during Sino-Japanese War, 1937–1945* (Vol. 1). Taipei: Academia Historica.

Lin, R.-J. (2014). *Transnational knowledge dissemination and re-contextualisation: The development of British educational foundation disciplines in Taiwan, 1968–2013* (Unpublished doctoral thesis). Institute of Education, University of London, London.

Liou, W.-C. (2007a). Reception and transformation of German Kulturpädagogik in China and its interpretation by Chinese scholars. *Bulletin of Educational Research, 53*, 93–127.

Liou, W.-C. (2007b). Knowledge transfer: The reception and transformation of German Pedagogy by Chinese educationists, 1928–1943. *Journal of Taiwan Normal University: Education, 52*, 43–64.

Liou, W.-C. (2008). A historical review on dissemination of German Pedagogy in China and Taiwan, 1928–1983. *Bulletin of Educational Research, 54*, 19–51.

Liou, W.-C. (2013). An analysis of doctoral dissertations from Chinese students at Teachers College, Columbia University, 1914–1929. *Bulletin of Educational Research, 59*(2), 1–48.

Liu, T.-C. (2005). *Nationalism and the development of the study of education in Modern China, 1897–1919* (Unpublished master's dissertation). Department of Education, National Taiwan Normal University, Taipei, Taiwan.

Liu, X.-Q. (2005). *The modern history of Chinese students studying in the UK*. Tianjin: The Nankai University.

Nitobe, I. (1931). Two exotic currents in Japanese civilisation. In I. Nitobe (Ed.), *Western influences in modern Japan: A series of papers on cultural relations* (pp. 1–24). Chicago, IL: University of Chicago Press & Japanese Council of the Institute of Pacific Relations.

Shu, X.-C. (1926). *The modern history of Chinese students studying abroad*. Shanghai: Shanghai Culture, 1926.

Shu, X.-C. (Ed.). (1989). *The history of student studying abroad in modern China*. Shanghai: Shanghai Culture.

Wang, I.-W. (2013). *The establishment of new school systems in Late Qing Dynasty: An analysis of the Japanese factors* (Unpublished master's dissertation). Department of Education, National Taiwan Normal University, Taipei, Taiwan.

Wei, D.-J. (Ed.). (1998). *A history of the academic exchange between China and foreign countries.* Changsha: Hunan Education.

Wright, M. C. (1957). *The last stand of Chinese conservatism: The Tung-Chih Restoration, 1862–1874.* Stanford, CA: The Stanford University Press.

Wu, M.-Y. (2005). Reconstructing the 1934–1937 debate over modern China's philosophy of education. *Bulletin of Educational Research, 51,* 27–51.

Wu, M.-Y. (2009). The reception of foreign educational thought by modern China, 1909–1948: An analysis in terms of Luhmannian selection and self-reference. *Paedagogica Historica, 45,* 309–328.

Xiao, Y.-M. (2002). The emergence of the discipline of educational studies in China. In L.-X. Gin (Ed.), *The development and reflection of the discipline of educational studies in the twentieth century in China* (pp. 16–63). Shanghai: Shanghai Education. 2002, 16–17.

Yamasaki, Y. (2010). The impact of Western progressive educational ideas in Japan: 1868–1940. *History of Education, 39,* 575–588.

Yan, J.-Q. (2002). *The use and transmission of Chinese culture in the eighteenth century in Western Europe.* Hangzhou: China Academy of Art Press.

Yoshida, K. (1931). European and American influences in Japanese education. In I. Nitobe (Ed.), *Western influences in modern Japan: A series of papers on cultural relations* (pp. 25–55). Chicago, IL: University of Chicago Press & Japanese Council of the Institute of Pacific Relations.

Zhang, C. (2002). *A comparative study on Eastern and Western culture: Matteo Ricci in China and other essays.* Hong Kong: City University of Hong Kong.

Zhou, G.-P. (1996). *The dissemination of modern Western educational theories in China.* Guangdong: Guangdong Education.

Learning from the Barbarians? Reflections on Chinese Identity and 'Race' in the Educational Context

HEKTOR K.T. YAN

Abstract

This paper takes a reflective look at the notions of identity, 'race' and ethnicity using a few ancient and modern Chinese 'texts'. It begins with an examination of the reforms known as 'adopting the costume of barbarian/foreign people and practicing mounted archery [hufuqishe]' carried out by King Wuling 武靈王 (in reign 325–299 BCE) in 307 BCE as described in the Zhan Guo Ce 戰國策 *and the* Shiji 史記 *by Sima Qian 司馬遷 (c.145-c.87 BCE). Its cultural and educational significance is then discussed in order to show how the issues faced by King Wuling are still relevant to the educational scene in the contemporary world. Some recent materials from Hong Kong school textbooks relating to the issues on identity and 'race' are then used to contrast and compare with the approach taken by King Wuling. This study argues that the inability to take a critical stance toward categories such as 'race' (zhongzu) risks perpetuating dated and ethically questionable mentalities. In addition, the importance of taking into consideration issues pertaining to purpose and evaluation in the context of education is highlighted.*

1. Prolog: Learning from the Barbarians?

King Wuling of Zhao (趙) is usually mentioned in history books and school textbooks as a king from the Warring States period (475–221 BCE) who carried out significant reforms in order to strengthen his state. Such reforms, commonly referred to as *hufuqishe* 胡服騎射 (literally 'barbarian/foreign costume mounted archery'), are often described as a significant feat that resulted in making Zhao an emerging military power toward the end of the Warring States period. However, a closer look at one of the sources where these events are recorded, the *Shiji* of Sima Qian, reveals a much more complicated story. In the first instance, one of the main criticisms against King

Wuling's aspiration was made not on purely military or strategic grounds, as Zhao Cheng argues:

> Your servant heard that the Middle Kingdom [*zhongguo*] is the place where the wise and intelligent live, where the multitude of things and wealths concentrate, where the sagely and saintly teach, where benevolence and righteousness are followed, where the classics of poetry and history, rituals and music are practiced, where extraordinary and ingenious skills are tested, where people from far away look up to, and where the barbarous and alien people perform their right deeds. Now your majesty is abandoning all these and tries to copy the costume from far away, this is going to make changes to the teaching from the past, alter the way of the ancients, and contravene the hearts of humans. Since all these amount to violations of learning [*xue*] and deviations from what belongs to the Middle Kingdom, your servant hopes that your majesty can reconsider everything. (My translation)[1]

For simplicity's sake, this paper does not attempt to address the question whether Sima Qian's description was an accurate representation of the events in 307 BCE. What can be discerned with certainty is this: the historical accounts available to us suggest that it makes sense to say that the reluctance on the part of the Zhao court to alter their costume stems from their own sense of identity. King Wuling's attempt to initiate changes in his state has another important dimension because his avowed plan to reform is meant to 'civilize' or 'educate' (*jiao* 教) his people. From this perspective, the Zhao court's response amounts to a refusal to 'learn' (*xue* 學) from the *hu* 胡, the 'foreigners' or 'barbarians'. To borrow contemporary language, one may say that this historical episode bears witness to the power relationships implicit among the debate concerning the theory of knowledge and what ought to be taught. In other words, the issues of what deserves to be seen as knowledge and what ought to be included in the curriculum lie at the heart of the dispute. As Michael W. Apple puts it: '[…] the decision to define some groups' knowledge as worthwhile to pass on to future generations while other groups' culture and history hardly see the light of day says something extremely important about who has power in society (2004, p. xx)'. While Apple highlights the fact that values can be passed on through the 'hidden curriculum' of an educational system, the records about King Wuling's decision to adopt the costume of the *hu* address the questions about knowledge and teaching in an explicit manner.[2]

Taking into consideration the above complications, the reform planned by King Wuling involved far more than a change in military outfit and fighting strategy: in addition to highlighting the prominence of education in ancient China,[3] important issues related to identity, the perception of one's culture and the educational ethos are at stake. As we are about to see from the discussion below, in response to the opposition, the king marshaled together a line of arguments that cover issues pertaining to the nature of rituals, customs, governance and other social institutions. In addition, he had to make manifest his own attitudes to past traditions and the necessity to adapt to changes. The restructuring introduced by King Wuling proved to be a far-reaching one in Chinese history: the utilization of elements of nomadic warfare shifted the balance of power between the sedentary populations and their nomadic neighbors. In the words of the historian Christoph Baumer:

> The value of well-trained mounted archers was again demonstrated in 244 BCE, when Zhao's general Li Mu first halted the advance of an enormous Xiongnu army with infantry and chariots, before attacking them from behind with 30,000 bowmen on horseback, whom he had been drilling for years, thus annihilating the enemy. The ruler of the Xiongnu, the chanyu, managed, with great difficulty, to escape, and [according to the *Zizhi tongjian* and the *Shiji*] 'for the next ten or more years the Xiongnu did not have the courage nor the strength to venture near the borders of Zhao'. (Baumer, 2014, p. 5)

Apart from its tactical values, the adaptation of mounted archery and the costume of the *hu* are clear indications that a complex relationship between the sedentary and nomadic populations already existed at the time. With this a variety of intriguing issues, pertaining to customs, identity and what it means for something to be 'common' and 'strange', emerges. Due to the fact that northern nomads such as the Xiongnu and the Mongols conquered parts or the whole of China, the tension created by differences in customs (from clothing to social institutions) between the Han and their nomadic conquerors can be seen throughout antiquity, right up to the Qing dynasty and modern day China.

The fear of losing one's ethnic identity is a recurring theme in Chinese history. An early ruler of the Manchus, Hong Taiji (1592–1643), warned thus:

> I have heard that among the nations that have accepted Heaven's charge and founded an enterprise [i.e. established a dynasty for ruling China], none has abandoned their own language and turned instead to use the language of another nation. No nations that have abandoned their own language and taken up another nation's language have prospered.

Hong Taiji's fear that the Manchus might lose their native language could no doubt be seen as a part of a cultural identity, where their way of life encompasses not just the linguistic dimension. This idea finds expression in another remark made by him: 'What I fear is this: that the children and grandchildren of later generations will abandon the Old Way [of the Manchus], neglect shooting and riding, and enter into the Chinese Way!' (Elliott, 2001, p. 9).

This paper uses King Wuling's reform in the *Shiji* as the basis for a discussion on Chinese identity, 'race', ethnicity and multiculturalism in the context of education. Following Paul Ricoeur, I treat the King Wuling episode, as recorded in historical texts, as a narrative. By focusing on how important ideas such as *jiao*, custom and identity are conceptualized in these ancient texts, I hope to 'open up the real towards the possible' and 'uncover the buried potentialities of the present' (Ricoeur, 1981, p. 295). In the next Section (2), I offer my reading of King Wuling's story with reference to the notions of identity, teaching/civilizing (*jiao*) and ethnic/racial categories. Some observations on the contemporary educational scene in Hong Kong will be used in Section 3 for contrast and comparison with the *hufuqishe* case. King Wuling's arguments, which bear important resemblances to contemporary multiculturalist thinking, can cast light on the importance of racial/ethnic categories in education. The discussion then brings to the fore the need to take into consideration issues of purpose. If education is a value-laden act in a non-incidental sense, it involves human intentions and decisions. This means that by its very nature education has a teleological dimension: it is performed by human beings for *some* purposes, even if such purposes are taken for granted or ill-defined. The failure to recognize this may reproduce or reinforce existing, oppressive power relationships in the society (Alcoff, 1993). This paper can therefore be seen as a response to one of Apple's theoretical objectives:

> [...] I want educators, particularly those specifically interested in what happens inside classrooms, to critically examine the assumptions they had about what education does. These assumptions concern some very deep seated, but often unconscious, pressuppositions about science, the nature of men and women, and the ethics and politics of our day-to-day curricular and pedagogic theories and practices. (Apple, 2004, p. xxi)

If education in the contemporary world is increasingly characterized by a mechanistic conception which objectifies both students and educators, it is crucial that educators should have a full understanding regarding the nature of their own practice. This requires that they become fully conscious of the inevitability of evaluation and making value judgements.[4]

2. Contextualization and Analysis

Sima Qian's account of King Wuling's reform begins with the king's awareness of the precarious condition of the state of Zhao. Having decided to adopt the costume of the 'barbarian' or 'foreigner' (*hufu*), the king discusses his plan with one of his ministers:

> The king says: '... now as I plan to wear the costumes of the *hu* and practice mounted archery in order to educate [*jiao*] the people, how can I deal with the inevitable scenario that the people will talk about my decision?' Feiyi [肥義] replies: 'Your servant heard that one cannot accomplish anything if one is indecisive, and one will never achieve good fame if one has doubts regarding what one does. If your majesty has decided to embark on what is contrary to the customs, then your majesty should not have any concern about the opinions of the people. Those who reflect on the great virtues are prepared to diverge from existing customs; those who attain great deeds need not deliberate with *hoi polloi*. In the past, Shun performed dance for the people of Youmiao; Yu exposed his body to enter the State of the Naked. These are not done in order to indulge in one's appetites or to please one's mind. Instead, these are undertakings to engage in the virtues and to achieve rewards. Since the stupid remain ignorant when a deed is over while the wise can comprehend it before it is done, why should your majesty have any doubt?' The king says: 'I do not have any doubt about the

costume of the *hu*, what I worry is that the people will laugh at me. [But] what is pleasurable to a madman is actually a misery to the wise; what is laughable to the stupid is scrutinized by the able person. If there are people in this world who obey me, there is no limit to the potential benefit by adopting the costume of the *hu*. Even if the whole world will laugh at me, it is by necessity that I can conquer the land of the *hu* and the state of Zhongshan [中山]'. (My translation)

The exchange between the king and Feiyi leaves us with the feeling that the planned reforms are intimately connected with what people then considered 'normal'. The references to the sage-kings Shun and Yu also stress that perceptions about cultural differences matter. Feiyi's support of the king encouraged him to wear the *hu* costume. The *Shiji* then turns to the king's attempt to persuade his uncle, Zhao Cheng 趙成 (also known as Gongzicheng 公子成), to wear the new costume. Zhao Cheng's opposition (quoted above in Section 1) hinges on the view that the *hu* costume is at variance with the type of costume common in the 'Middle Kingdom' (*zhongguo*). This observation is itself premised on the perceived radical distinctions between what characterizes the *zhongguo* and what characterizes the 'barbarous and alien' [*manyi* 蠻夷]: here the Middle Kingdom (which was at the time of King Wuling a loose collection of feudal states) is held as a paragon of what is excellent in cultural, technological and ethical terms. Whether this view itself is persuasive is of course questionable, it is still apparent that the underlying sentiment presupposes a strong sense of distinct identity. For, without such a sense of identity, the refusal to copy and follow foreign custom would not make sense. This mentality is itself consistent with a remark found in the *Mencius*, which reports Mencius as saying that 'I have heard of using Xia customs to transform the Yi, but I have never heard of being transformed by the Yi. [吾聞用夏變夷者，未聞變於夷者也]' (*Mencius*, 3A4, trans. Bloom, 2009, p. 58).

In responding to his challengers, the king employs a number of different strategies. Among other things, he points out that the political situation and the geographical location of the state of Zhao create an urgent need for mounted archers. First and foremost, King Wuling is keen to dispute his opponents' view on costume and their sense of what is fitting: he states that the purpose of costume lies in its being conducive to practice needs. In a similar vein, he also posits that the purpose of ritual consists in its being expedient. In short, the king believes that costumes and rituals need not be uniform or unchanging, so long as they can respond to the circumstances of particular place and time:

> Costume is created with its use in mind, rituals are set up to make our deeds effortless. The sages introduce appropriate measures by observing the people and set up rituals according to circumstances: these are done for the purpose of enriching the state and benefiting the people. Having short hair, tattoos, exposing their shoulders with robes opening to the left: these distinguish the people of Ouyue. Blackening the teeth, pricking one's forehead, wearing fish-skin hats and rough clothing characterize the customs of the great state of Wu. It can be seen from these examples that although ritual

and costume are not the same everywhere, they share the purpose of being expedient. A change in location alters their usage; a change in circumstances modifies the rituals. In considering what can be beneficial to his state, the sage does not resort to only one method. What can be serviceable to his deeds need not match the sage's own rituals. [...] Being impartial and charitable requires one not to be mistrustful when one is dealing with something one does not understand, and not to be dismissive towards what is different from oneself. (My translation)

King Wuling's exchanges with his ministers show that the underlying concern of the dispute seems to lie less in the use of mounted archery than in changing their existing costume. The *Zhan Guo Ce*, which contains a version of King Wuling's story, offers extra textual evidence in this regard. One follower of the king puts his condemnation this way:

The customs which sustain us today are the ways of antiquity. Proper clothing is an injunction of propriety. That observation of the law must not err is known to all your people. These three facts were what our former sages taught [*jiao*] us (Trans. Crump, 1996, p. 292).

Another critic of the king points out that:

Barbarian clothing [*hufu*] is not thought well of in the world and wearing it would not be something that would instruct people [*jiaomin*] and make the proprieties complete. If the garment be outlandish, intentions become disordered; when custom is flouted, the people become rebellious. So it is that one who rules a country does not clothe himself in strange garments. The Middle Kingdoms [*zhongguo*] have no affinity for barbarian [*manyi*] activities, so this action of yours is not something which teaches the people [*jiaomin*] and makes the proprieties complete. (Trans. Crump, 1996, p. 293)

In response to this kind of criticism, King Wuling reiterates his opinion that social practices such as the law and related customs such as costumes and rituals need not be fixed: they have to change over time and be responsive to circumstances. To counter the claim that strange and unusual costumes give rise to unruly behavior, the king's answer amounts to nothing less than an early statement of multiculturalism:

If whimsical costumes create indulgence, then it would be the case that there is no eccentric behaviour in the lands of Zou and Lu. If unusual customs breed vulgarity, then it would be the case that there are no exceptional people among the Wu and Yue. [...] That's why the proverb says: 'Those who drive a chariot by following the instructions from a book do not understand what the horses are like; those who use the way of the past to remake the present do not understand that the state-of-affairs has changed'. (My translation)

By insisting that what is considered to be acceptable conduct is not to be found exclusively among some specific, culturally-defined groups, King Wuling's reply mirrors contemporary controversies concerned with multiculturalism. As Rattansi (2011) has forcefully demonstrated, the recent disinclination toward multicultural policies in Western countries (such as Germany and Britain) does not attest to the fact that a post-multicultural era has arrived or that viable alternatives to multiculturalism are being implemented. Instead, an inability to follow multiculturalism often signals a regression to racist or ethnocentric thinking: the resistance to multiculturalism, therefore, has an undertone based on racialization. Analogously, the inability to accept the possibilities that one's out-group or people with 'strange' customs can exhibit good qualities is a likely indicator of racism.

From this perspective, the King Wuling episode can be seen to be relevant to the contemporary world in many ways.[5] First of all, King Wuling's rhetoric can be seen to be in sharp contrast to one 'essentialist' view which maintains that there are radical and entrenched differences between what is *hu* and what is 'Chinese' (or what belongs to *zhongguo*).[6] Second, the controversy surrounding the desirability of *hu* costume not only highlights the transformative possibilities when one pays attention to role of purpose, it also offers us a clear example of the interplay between power, identity and culture. The exchanges between King Wuling and his ministers do not only touch on issues relating to the politics of identity, they are also relevant to important concepts in education such as teaching, learning, civilizing and legitimizing. Just as the introduction of minority cultures in the curriculum can be a controversial topic in liberal, multi-cultural societies, the adaptation of 'barbarian' or 'foreign' costume can also be a thorny issue in ancient China. In the contemporary world, changes in one's custom or way of living can be seen as a threat to one's identity: the *hidjab* is one example. In the school context, while the inclusion of minority cultures in the syllabus may help members of such cultures to preserve their distinct way of life, the same move could be seen by members of the dominant group as eroding their cherished tradition (Tamir, 2003).

The case of King Wuling also draws our attention to the content of identity formation. While language and descent are often considered to be significant components of one's identity, there seems to be no fixed way to delineate what might or might not be used in the construction of one's identity. As the debate between the king and his followers shows, although the desire to identify oneself as belonging to the 'Middle Kingdom' can be a strong one, the option of adopting the customs of the *hu* is still available. In other words, the use of the category *hu* as the Other to define the Self turns out to be contingent: what belongs to the Other can be incorporated into 'one's own'.

3. A Comparison with Contemporary Materials

A comparative look at contemporary educational materials in current Hong Kong in light of the historical narrative surrounding King Wuling's reform will provide us with opportunities to discern the possibilities of continuity and change. At this juncture, we are going to look at some concrete, particular examples pertaining to how identity is actually conceptualized and presented in school textbooks. As textbooks and other teaching materials are by nature accepted texts which are considered to be authoritative, their use in the discussion here has a *prima facie* advantage that they embody and represent commonsensical opinions and sentiments. In what follows, I want to show that a brief look at such materials can make plain the fact that the contemporary Chinese (or Hong Kong) identity seems to bear signs of being essentialized: despite a self-perceived need to accommodate a more open and inclusive society, a racialized notion of being 'Chinese' seems to be present.[7] The discussion will then be followed by an examination of the implications.

The fact that 'Chineseness' has been constructed through its Other is a well-documented phenomenon. A tendency to see what belongs to the 'Middle Kingdom' as civilized and the readiness to associate the non-Chinese with a lack of culture has already taken root since antiquity. This notion of Chinese superiority, which finds expression in the very idea of the 'Middle Kingdom' suggests the model of center-periphery thinking. This is further reinforced by a notion of a common descent shared by the whole Chinese population. In a recent textbook on Liberal Studies [通識教育 *tongshijiaoyu*], this idea is still applied to characterize the Chinese (or *Hua* descent [*huayi*] 華裔) and the population of Hong Kong:

> Most Hongkongers are Chinese. They share a common lineage [*xieyuan*, literally "blood relation"] with the residents in Mainland China, both are descendants of Yan and Yellow Emperors... [香港人口大部分是華裔，血緣上與內地居民同屬炎黃子孫...]. (Xu, 2012, p. 224, my translation)

One could easily dismiss this rather bizarre reference to two mythical emperors by pointing out that this piece of information is virtually unfalsifiable. However, from the perspective of narrative, it is hard to over-estimate the importance of such a move. The mere act of asserting a common descent serves a fundamental need on the part of human beings to trace their origin. By placing the two emperors as the ancestors of one's group, a sense of structure or narrative 'order' is obtained: this not only gives closure to the need to track one's origin from the distant past, the identification of one's ancestors serves the function of creating a shared identity by homogenizing one's own group.[8] This way of identity formation not only has an exclusive element, it also suggests the presence of 'racialization', namely, the process whereby identity is taken to be based on biological features which are perceived as innate and immutable.

Another example taken from a textbook bears witness to the above suspicion. Having stated that 'identity is multidimensional', the author of this Liberal Studies textbook proceeds to discuss various elements constituting one's identity:

> Identity can be related to various dimensions. Everyone has different positions and roles in relation to domains such as the family, religion, state, nation and workplace, and this can create multiple identities. The constitution of one's identity can have different elements, they can be divided into the following according to their nature:

- Ascribed status: Inherent, such as gender, race and ancestral home; identities constituted by these elements are relatively stable.
- Achieved status: Acquirable, such as profession, academic achievement and mem-

bership in [public] interest groups; identities constituted by these elements are relatively mobile, they can be changed by time and the surrounding environment. (Wu, Huang, & Huang, 2012, p. 209, my translation)

Here, 'race' (*zhongzu* 種族),[9] together with gender and ancestral home (*jiguan* 籍貫) are used as examples to clarify the concept of 'ascribed status'. While 'ascribed status' is considered to be 'inherent' or 'in-born' (*yushengjulaide* 與生俱來的) and is said to be a relatively 'stable' dimension of an identity, an 'achieved status' such as profession and academic achievement is deemed to be able 'to be changed over time and places'. Understood thus, 'race' is perceived to have an objective status, comparable to observable biological traits, and it can therefore be imposed on an individual with or without the consent of the individual involved.

In the following passage from the textbook by Xu (2012), the connection between 'race' (understood as part of 'nature') and human behavior (as part of 'culture') is made clear:

> Race [*zhongzu*] and lineage [*xieyuan*] are something inborn and immutable to human beings. This is why some schools of thought think that one's identity is based on some testable and objective characteristics such as race, lineage and language. Due to such compatriotic relationships (*tongbaoguanxi* 同胞關係), which involve a common ancestor and ancestral home (*tongzongtongzu* 同宗同族), people will have some common cultural characteristics such as the same language, custom and similar values, and they will therefore care about each other, and have stronger feelings towards the groups which share the same ancestral home or lineage. Examples of these include stronger loyalty, care and a sense of belonging. [These also result in] the willingness to participate in the affairs within the group. [These are done] with the aim that through such undertakings, one may develop one's personal identity and identity-recognition. (Xu, 2012, p. 224, my translation)

Implicit in these two examples is the assumption that 'race' is something observable and that it is relatively 'stable' when compared with indicators of identity such as profession and academic achievement. It is even described as 'objective'. The fact that there is no explicit explanation as to which 'schools of thought' actually endorse this notion of 'race' is particularly revealing: it seems likely that the author of the textbook is simply reproducing what she considers to be a commonsensical way of thinking. At the same time, the examples betray the view that a person's 'race' has some objective and scientific basis. The widespread view, especially among social scientists, that there is no sound scientific and biological basis in support of biological races, is not mentioned in the textbook. Due to the fact that the author of the textbook has posited that there is a interrelation between 'race' and a person's values and emotional attachments, the implication that a person's identity and ethical outlook are ultimately rooted in his or her 'race' or descent follows. This readiness to assign special value to one's in-group at the expense of one's out-group is consistent with a view which can be found in ancient China, as an oft-quoted passage from the *Zuozhuan* (左傳) reads:

'He/she who is not of our kind, his must have a different mind. [*feiwozulei, qixinbiyi* 非我族類，其心必異]'.

A number of different explanations, such as the prevalence of traditional biological racism or the influence of modern nationalism, could be employed to make sense of the ideas underlying the textbook passages discussed above. What I want to bring into focus is a lack of concern regarding the significance of *purpose*: the example from the *Shiji* suggests that although one's identity can be made up of contingent components such as rituals and costumes, such components are ultimately regarded as means to some further end. The realization that such practices have a purpose allows one to discard the impression that they are natural or inevitable, thus enabling critical questioning. At this point, some important issues concerning the notion of 'race' itself need to be raised. For what purpose is 'race' included in the curriculum? Is it a 'given' and immutable characteristic of humans or is it something comparable to one's costume? In his book *Injustice: Why social inequality persists*, Daniel Dorling offers the following remarks:

> Racism is the belief in the superiority of a particular race. A race is seen as a major division of humanity, a group of people connected by common descent. Traditionally racism has been targeted at a series of people who were seen to have their common descent revealed by the colour of their skin, facial features or language, but any group treated with disdain because they are seen as connected by common descent can become the subject of racism. (Dorling, 2011, p. 205)

Due to the fact that the notions of descent and 'race' are categories used to divide human beings into distinct groups, their usage in the educational context deserves scrutiny. Just as the division of humanity into two sexes or genders can be used in different contexts to justify a great variety of claims (some of them ethically suspect), it is clear that the use of categories necessarily involves evaluation and purpose (Root, 1993, pp. 149–172). While the talk of a common descent creates an impression of homogeneity, its corollary is that the absence of a common descent implies heterogeneity and hence a lack of 'cohesion' or 'social harmony'. Despite the fact that 'race' as a concept is often fluid in its usage, it has a basic function of putting human beings into discrete groups: this in itself can be used to fabricate expectations regarding what different 'races' should do or to justify normative claims made about members of different 'races'. In this way, certain practices are normalized or legitimized.

The possibility that one may be able to use certain methods to identify one's 'race' objectively and scientifically may appear to be able to settle the question. However, this is an illusion: granted, however unlikely, that there could be means to ascertain a human being's 'racial' make-up objectively and scientifically, the importance of this 'racial' data remains to be seen. Just as it is possible to argue that mounted archery is an *objective* cultural feature of certain nomadic people, this objective finding alone is silent about the significance of this practice. Without considering one's own practical purposes or ethical needs, one can still be clueless as to whether one should embrace it or not. This signals that, in attempting to understand how identity can be tied up (sometimes arbitrarily) with a certain set of characteristics, it is essential to address questions of meaning.

In this context, it is tempting to characterize the contemporary cultural climate as a scientistic one and use this to explain why 'race' as a disputed scientific concept still enjoys widespread currency in our society nowadays. What is scientistic here can simply refer to the readiness to *redefine* an issue in scientific terms (Scruton, 2015, pp. 136–137): the move to understand identity solely in 'scientific' terms such as 'race' and genes to the exclusion of other more 'value-laden' concepts such as culture or social transaction can therefore be seen as scientistic. The habitual refusal to grapple with issues of purpose and values in mainstream scientific inquiry further contributes to obscure the social and political functions of the term 'race' in everyday life.

While the above examples indicate that racialization may be taking place in the discussion of identity among some school textbooks, the overall picture is actually more ambiguous. In another textbook discussion of the topic of identity among the population of Hong Kong, the following passage can be found:

> In terms of lifestyle and culture, since Hong Kong has its own culture, people can be considered to be Hongkongers (*xianggangren*) in terms of lifestyle and culture as long as they have got used to living in Hong Kong; so a possible consequence of this is that these people need not be Hong Kong residents in the legal sense, but regarding their lifestyle and culture they are 'Hongkongers'. In general, 'Hongkoners' refer to those who treat Hong Kong as their home, those who have a sense of belonging to Hong Kong and those who believe that they are part of Hong Kong: these people are all 'Hongkongers'. (Feng, 2009, p. 205, my translation)

What we have got here is the co-existence of two opposing narratives. On the one hand, there is a narrative focusing on certain characteristics such as descent and lineage. According to this narrative, such characteristics are understood to be observable and verifiable (at least in principle). This makes possible the attribution of identity *without* paying attention to social perception and signification. On the other hand, the passage quoted above seems to hint at a counter-narrative where a person's own decision can play a legitimate role in identity formation. Concerning the first narrative, one may say that it signals a failure to fully take into account the *social* and *cultural* nature of identity formation. All observable or imagined traits could be attributed to individuals or groups: as such, their social meaning or significance remains unknown. It is only through a study of social interaction among particular human beings that it is possible to discern which differences are actually used to differentiate human beings from one another. The case of King Wuling can therefore be understood with reference to the counter-narrative: a perceived need to innovate the military and a particular understanding of the role of culture seem to work together to clarify the *meaning* behind the use of categories such as the 'foreign' or the 'barbarian'. From this perspective, despite the fact that the story about King Wuling dates back to antiquity, it possesses the ability to 'uncover the buried potentialities of the present'. At the same time, it can be used to remind us that human cultures are not always homogeneous or monolithic. Instead, cultures possess conflicts, rebellions and contestations of norms that originate from within or without: in this sense they evolve over time.[10] From this perspective, one must recognize the fact that a particular way of representing a culture or narrating the past is an exercise of power. For, how one's culture or one's past is conceptualized gives shape to one's perception of what is and what is not possible. In order to actively question essentialist and misconceived notions of culture and identity, an educator must problematize dominant and normalized narratives within the curriculum. In addition, to make room for meaningful alternatives, counter-narratives need to be explored and studied seriously.

4. Concluding Remarks

This paper begins with a discussion of the controversies triggered by the adaptation of '*hu* costume and mounted archery' where a number of issues and important concepts have been identified. The relevance of these issues and concepts to education is further examined with reference to some textbook materials in current Hong Kong. In short, the discussion aims to show how concepts such as identity, culture and learning interact with one another when they are fully contextualized. King Wuling's reform, as told by the authors of *Shiji* and *Zhan Guo Ce*, provides us with a perspective which clarifies, in a critical manner, the relationships between custom and identity. By contrast, the Hong Kong textbook materials discussed in this paper seem to exhibit a lack of such critical awareness. The controversial notion of 'race' is perceived to be commonsensical and included in the curriculum pertaining to identity. King Wuling's case can therefore serve to remind us that the construction of one's identity by employing 'race' is definitely not inevitable: it has the role of a counter-narrative.

The notion of 'race', when unquestioned, can give the impression of fulfilling a number of different tasks: it can not only satisfy humans' deep-seated need to address questions of origins, it can also function to create social legitimization by fabricating the appearance of homogeneity or irreconcilable differences. Its import in education can hardly be over-emphasized. From the discussion in this article, the risks associated with the use of the notion of 'race' in the context of education have been identified. When the notion of 'race' is introduced casually in textbooks in passing, its potential to mislead is greatest. This is because when 'race' is presented as a commonsensical notion, critical thoughts targeting it are inadvertently marginalized. In this sense, 'race' can be readily used for ideological purposes. As Brenda Cohen comments: 'the more free a society is from cruder indoctrinatory practices, the more important becomes recognition of the more subtle ways in which indoctrination can manifest itself (Bailey, 2010, p. 141 citing Cohen, 1981, p. 50)'. If an uncritical usage of the notion of 'race' can perpetuate certain ideas while sidelining certain others, it can be rightly seen as an example of unintentional indoctrination.

The historical narratives recording the venture of King Wuling prove to be useful in providing us with a concrete picture regarding the interplay between custom and identity. In it we get a glimpse of how constructed boundaries defining the Self and Other can be overcome when radical rethinking about the fundamental issues of purpose is carried out. This need to tackle purpose, which is also essential in ethical reasoning, seems to be inconspicuous in a culture dominated by scientific reasoning. I have tried to argue that this lack of attention to purpose when dealing with the notion of 'race' both naturalizes it and obscures its social functions. All these hint at the possibility that identity formation does not take place in a vacuum. Instead, the best hope for us to understand the working of identity may require an examination of a concrete situation where power is contested and exercised.

The awareness that human customs or practices such as rituals or costumes may serve some human purposes clarifies the distinction between natural events and human actions: while natural events can be predicted or manipulated through a study of the underlying causal mechanisms, human actions cannot be understood by resorting to causal mechanisms alone. To make sense of a human action, one must refer to the intention or purpose involved. While this is not a novel view to the students of the humanities and the social sciences, the educational resources needed for one to think through such issues are not always apparent. Granted that serious thought about purpose is often needed, one may still say that the alleged purposes of rituals or the concept of 'race' are far from clear. Here the issues concerned are philosophical in nature so the position of the teacher may become delicate: the invitation to investigate the purpose of human institutions and other social constructs may force some students to retreat into relativistic positions, but it may also have the advantage of creating the opportunity to engage in controversial discussions.

Acknowledgement

I would like to express my gratitude to Chun-Kit Chui for kindly sharing his research findings on Hong Kong textbooks. In addition, I would like to thank Samantha Wray for her support and advice. This paper has also benefited from the useful and constructive comments of the anonymous reviewers.

Disclosure statement

No potential conflict of interest was reported by the author.

Notes

1. In preparing my translation of the passages from the *Shiji*, I have consulted Han (2010), Pei, Sima, and Zhang (1982), Sima (1994) and Wang (1983). The *Zhan Guo Ce* (or *Chan-kuo Ts'e*) contains a version of King Wuling's story and it has been translated into English (Crump, 1996, pp. 288–294).
2. For a discussion on the relationship between knowledge and what is teachable, see Holland (1980, pp. 10–25).
3. The fact that these concepts emerged in this particular context attests to the importance given to education in ancient China. In the essay 'Record on the Subject of Education [學記 *Xue Ji*]', which forms part of an early Confucian text known as the *Liji* (禮記), it is stated that: 'Only if the Junzi can understand what is difficult and what is easy in perfecting learning and understand what is beautiful and ugly about it, then it is possible that the Junzi can use metaphor(s) to give a variety of examples [in teaching]. If the Junzi can use metaphor(s) to give a variety of examples [in teaching], then the Junzi can be a teacher. If the Junzi can be a teacher, then the Junzi can be a leader. If the Junzi can be a leader, then the Junzi can be a ruler. This is why learning to be a ruler starts from the teacher'. (My transla-

tion) See also the *Analects* 19.13 (Yang, 1958, p. 209): 'Having fulfilled his duty, the official should study. Having fulfilled his duty, the scholar should become an official. [仕而優則學, 學而優則仕]' The intimate connection between the positions of the official (*shi* 仕) and the scholar (*shi* 士) can be discerned from the characters themselves: they share a common radical and they are homophones.
4. Cf. Nevo (2013, p. 270): 'If the public is the medium through which relations of power are regulated in a given society, and there are better and worse ways of organizing such relations, society is clearly benefitted by scholarly disciplines in which the terms of these power relations are subordinated to a critical study, and in which the human reality of such power relations is expressed and clarified in a participatory, non-objectifying manner'.
5. The story of King Wuling, as recounted in the *Shiji* and *Zhan Guo Ce*, can be seen as a clear case of an *agon*: 'The agon, or conflict, has been so central a feature of narrative throughout its recorded history that it is reasonable to assume that it serves important cultural purposes. One very plausible possibility is that the representation of conflict in narrative provides a way for a culture to talk to itself about, and possibly resolve, conflicts that threaten to fracture it (or at least make living difficult). In this view of narrative, its conflicts are not solely about particular characters (or entities). Also in conflict, and riding on top of the conflict of narrative entities, are conflicts regarding values, ideas, feelings, and ways of seeing the world. There is, of course, no culture without many such conflicts. Narrative may, then, play an important social role as a vehicle for making the case for one side or another in a conflict, or for negotiating the claims of the opposing sides, or simply for providing a way for people to live with a conflict that is irreconcilable (as, for example, the conflict between the desire to live and the knowledge that we have to die)' (Abbott, 2008, p. 55).
6. Cf. Cobley (2014, p. 37): '[…] narrative does not reveal universality; rather it has been instrumental in the promotion of difference, helping to preserve some memories and not others, and helping to bind some people into a given community and not others. In fact, narrative has sometimes assisted in upholding an absolutist conception of cultural difference, especially in its contribution to the concept of tradition'.
7. For a recent look at 'race' in the Chinese context, see Cheng (2011). The question whether 'race' has a sound basis in biology is an on-going one. On this issue, see, for example, Glasgow (2010) and Sesardic (2010).
8. The reference to Emperors Yan and Huang ('Yellow') appeared recently in Ma Ying-jeou's speech during his meeting with Xi Jinping on 7 November 2015.
9. For a discussion of *zhongzu* in the Chinese context, see Dikötter (2002).
10. See Nussbaum (1997), especially Chapter Four.

References

Abbott, H. P. (2008). *The Cambridge introduction to narrative* (2nd ed.). Cambridge: Cambridge University Press.
Alcoff, L. (1993). How is epistemology political? In R. S. Gottlieb (Ed.), *Radical philosophy: Tradition, counter-tradition, politics* (pp. 65–85). Philadelphia, PA: Temple University Press.
Apple, M. W. (2004). *Ideology and curriculum* (3rd ed.). New York, NY: Routledge.

Bailey, R. (2010). What's wrong with indoctrination and brainwashing? In R. Bailey (Ed.), *The philosophy of education: An introduction* (pp. 136–146). London: Continuum.

Baumer, C. (2014). *The history of Central Asia: The age of the silk roads*. London: I. B. Tauris.

Bloom, I. (Trans.). (2009). *Mencius*. New York, NY: Columbia University Press.

Cheng, Y. (2011). From campus racism to cyber racism: Discourse of race and Chinese nationalism. *The China Quarterly, 207*, 561–579.

Cobley, P. (2014). *Narrative* (2nd ed.). New York, NY: Routledge.

Cohen, B. (1981). *Education and the individual*. London: Unwin.

Crump, J. I. (Trans.). (1996). *Chan-kuo Ts'e* (Revised ed.). Ann Arbor: Center for Chinese Studies, The University of Michigan.

Dikötter, F. (2002). Race in China. In D. T. Goldberg & J. Solomos (Eds.), *A companion to racial and ethnic studies* (pp. 495–510). Malden, MA: Blackwell.

Dorling, D. (2011). *Injustice: Why social inequality persists*. Bristol: The Policy Press.

Elliott, M. C. (2001). *The Manchu way: The eight banners and ethnic identity in late imperial China*. Stanford, CA: Stanford University Press.

Feng, R. 馮潤儀 (2009). *Gaozhongxinshijitongshi danyuan 2 jinrixianggang*, 高中新世紀通識 單元 2 今日香港. Hong Kong 香港: Ling Kee.

Glasgow, J. (2010). Another look at the reality of race, by which I mean racef. In A. Hazlett, (Eds.) *New waves in metaphysics* (pp. 54–71). Basingstoke: Palgrave Macmillan.

Han, Z. (Trans.). (2010). *Shi ji* 史記. Beijing Shi 北京市: Zhonghua shu ju 中华书局.

Holland, R. F. (1980). *Against empiricism: On education, epistemology and value*. Oxford: Blackwell.

Nevo, I., (Yanni) (2013). The ethics of humanistic scholarship: On knowledge and acknowledgement. *Journal of the Philosophy of History, 7*, 266–298.

Nussbaum, M. C. (1997). *Cultivating humanity: A classical defense of reform in liberal education*. Cambridge: Harvard University Press.

Pei, Y. 裴駰, Sima, Z. 司馬貞, & Zhang, S. 張守節 (Eds.). (1982). *Shi ji* 史記 (2nd ed.). Beijing 北京: Zhonghua shu ju 中華書局.

Sima, Q. 司馬遷. (1994). *Shi ji: wen bai dui zhao* 史記：文白對照, *Yinchuan shi* 銀川市: *Ningxia ren min chu ban she* 寧夏人民出版社.

Rattansi, A. (2011). *Multiculturalism*. Oxford: Oxford University Press.

Ricoeur, P. (1981). *Hermeneutics and the human sciences: Essays on language, action, and interpretation*. Edited, translated, and introduced by J. B. Thompson. Cambridge: Cambridge University Press.

Root, M. (1993). *Philosophy of social science: The methods, ideals and politics of social inquiry*. Oxford: Blackwell.

Scruton, R. (2015). Scientism and the humanities. In R. N. Williams & D. N. Robinson (Eds.), *Scientism: The new orthodoxy* (pp. 131–146). London: Bloomsbury Academic.

Sesardic, N. (2010). Race: A social destruction of a biological concept. *Biology & Philosophy, 25*, 143–162.

Tamir, Y. (2003). Education and the politics of identity. In R. Curren (Ed.), *A companion to the philosophy of education* (pp. 501–508). Malden, MA: Blackwell.

Wang, S. (1983). *Shi ji jiao zheng* 史記斠證, *Taibei* 台北: *Zhong yang yan jiu yuan li shi yu yan yan jiu suo* 中央研究院歷史語言研究所.

Wu, L. 吳麗芳, Huang, M. 黃明樂, & Huang, T. 黃天賜. (2012). *Yajixingaozhongtongshijiaoyu* 雅集新高中通識教育. Hong Kong 香港: Aristo Educational Press.

Xu, D. 許戴美霞. (2012). *Xinshiyetongshijiaoyu jinrixianggang (zongheban)* 新視野通識教育 今日香港 (綜合版). Hong Kong 香港: Hong Kong Educational Publishing 香港教育圖書公司.

Yang, B. 楊伯峻 (Trans.). (1958). *Lun yu yi zhu* 論語譯注. Beijing 北京: Zhonghua shu ju 中華書局.

Confucius: Philosopher of twenty-first century skills

LEONARD TAN

Abstract

In this article, I examine the Partnership for twenty-first Century Skills (P21) framework from a Confucian perspective. Given that this framework has attracted attention around the world, including Confucian-heritage societies, an analysis of how key ideas compare with Confucian values appears important and timely. As I shall show, although Confucian philosophy largely resonates with the 'Learning and Innovation Skills' in the P21 framework, namely, critical thinking, communication, collaboration and creativity, it also provides fresh perspectives and nuances the framework. These insights include the notion that critical thinking is not a strictly cognitive endeavour but an affective one as well, a social construal of the self, and an ethical notion of creativity. This article aims to redress the under-representation of Asian philosophy in the philosophy of education. It also hopes to initiate more philosophical dialogues between Asia and the West.

Educational discourse in recent years has increasingly centred on the much-touted 'twenty-first century skills' that aim to prepare students to meet the challenges and demands of contemporary society (e.g. Binkley et al., 2012; European Parliament & the Council of the European Union, 2007; National Research Council, 2012; Partnership for 21st Century Skills, 2009a, 2009b; Trilling & Fadel, 2009). These skills have attracted much attention around the world (Ananiadou & Claro, 2009; Voogt & Roblin, 2012), including 'Confucian-heritage' societies (Niu, 2012, p. 274; Starr, 2012, p. 17) such as Mainland China, Taiwan, Japan, Korea and Singapore. This raises the following questions: How do the twenty-first century skills resonate with Confucian ideas? How might Confucian philosophy contribute to a twenty-first century approach to education in this present globalised world?

In this philosophical comparative analysis, I examine the twenty-first century skills from Confucian lenses. In particular, I draw on three major Confucian texts—the *Analects* ('collected sayings' or *lunyu* 論語), the *Zhongyong* (中庸: 'Doctrine of the Mean'), and the *Daxue* (大學: 'the Great Learning')—to show how Confucian philosophy resonates with the 'Learning and Innovation Skills' in the influential 'Partnership for twenty-first Century' (P21) framework (Trilling & Fadel, 2009). These skills, often known as the four 'C's (i.e. critical thinking, communication, collaboration and creativity), are important and worthy of study because they are 'the keys to unlocking a lifetime of learning and creative work' (Trilling & Fadel, 2009, p. 49). In addition to showing resonances between Confucian philosophy and the P21 framework, I also illustrate how the philosophical ideas of Confucius may enhance ideas articulated by Trilling and Fadel. In the sections that ensue, I discuss the four 'C's in turn.

Critical Thinking

In their discussion of critical thinking, one argument Trilling and Fadel (2009) forwarded was that in 'every subject, at every grade level, instruction and learning must include commitment to a knowledge core, high demands on thinking, and active use of knowledge' (p. 50). As I shall show, all three aspects are prominent in Confucian philosophy.

For Trilling and Fadel (2009), 'commitment to a knowledge core' is crucial to critical thinking. Citing Resnick and Hall (1998), they argue that 'just as facts do not constitute true knowledge and thinking power, so thinking processes cannot proceed without something to think about' (p. 50). The futility of thinking 'without something to think about' can be seen in how Confucius laments that he once engaged in thought (*si* 思) for an entire day without eating and an entire night without sleeping, but it did no good. Instead, it would have been better had he 'spent that time in learning (*xue* 學)' (*Analects* 15.31; Slingerland, 2003, p. 186). For Confucius, it is important to learn a knowledge core of the classical texts, such as the *Odes* or the *Shijing* (詩經), a collection of three hundred songs and poems sung at religious and court ceremonies in early China (*Analects* 3.8, 13.5 and 17.9). Without such a core, there is no basis for one to think clearly (Slingerland, 2003). In fact, Confucius goes so far as to say that one who does not learn the *Odes* is 'like someone standing with his face to the wall' (*Analects* 17.10; Slingerland, 2003, p. 204. See also *Analects* 16.13).

While thinking (*si* 思) without learning (*xue* 學) a knowledge core leads to one being 'lost', learning without thinking leads to 'danger' (學而不思則罔, 思而不學則殆) (*Analects* 2.15; Slingerland, 2003, p. 13;. See also, the *Xunzi*: 1/1/12). This Confucian emphasis on thinking resonates with Trilling and Fadel's call for educators to place 'high demands on thinking' in education at all levels. For Trilling and Fadel (2009), learning is not about mere rote memorisation, but the ability to 'ask significant questions that clarify various points of view and lead to better solutions' (p. 52). This is emphasised in the Confucian texts, where Confucius himself often asks questions (*Analects* 3.15), is persistent in his questioning (*Analects* 9.8), and expects his students to question and even contradict what he teaches (*Analects* 2.9). In addition, it is important for Trilling and Fadel (2009) that students are able to 'synthesise and make connections between information and arguments' (p. 52). This recalls a dialogue where Confucius asks his disciple Zigong if he sees him as a person who studies a great deal and remembers it all. Zigong says, 'Yes. Is this not the case?' And

Confucius replies, 'It is not. I bind it all together with a single thread (*yiguan* 一貫)' (*Analects* 15.3; Slingerland, 2003, p. 174). As Kim (2003) argues, such 'binding' is 'cognitive in nature, and requires attending to underlying principles or roots in a critical manner' (p. 83). Confucius does not merely memorise, but analyses, interprets, evaluates, summarises and synthesises what he learns, all of which are important aspects of critical thinking.

In addition, Trilling and Fadel's efforts to dispel aspects of the famous 'Bloom's Taxonomy' resonates with the 2500-year-old tradition of Confucian philosophy. For Trilling and Fadel (2009), 'the lockstep, one-before-the-other learning sequence that teachers have been taught in education schools' that leads from 'knowledge, then comprehension, then application, then analysis, then synthesis, and finally evaluation' has been 'shattered by decades of accumulated research that proves this is not how students really learn most effectively–or in many cases, not how they learn at all' (p. 51). No such rigid sequence of learning is found in the classical Confucian texts. The Chinese word for thinking, *si* (思), is a broad term that 'encompasses a range of thought processes such as understanding, reflection, analysis, synthesis, evaluation, making connections, drawing analogies, making inferences, forming judgments and so on'—it is a 'taxonomy of thinking' (Tan, 2015, pp. 430–431). While Confucian philosophy stresses the importance of deep learning, reflecting on what one has learned, and the so-called 'higher-order thinking skills' in Bloom's taxonomy, it does not construe them in a rigidly hierarchical manner.

Having shown how Confucian philosophy resonates with Trilling and Fadel's call for twenty-first education to focus on a 'knowledge core' and place 'high demands on thinking', I turn now to the third aspect, that is, 'active use of knowledge'. This is seen very clearly when Confucius declares that 'If people can recite all of the three hundred Songs and yet when given official responsibility, fail to perform effectively … what good are they?' (*Analects* 13.5; Ames & Rosement, 1998, p. 163). For Confucius, commitment to a knowledge core and thinking about them are not enough; it is crucial to use the knowledge. Similarly, the *Zhongyong* exhorts us to 'study the way (*dao* 道) broadly, ask about it in detail, reflect on it carefully, analyse it carefully, and advance on it with earnestness' (Ames & Hall, 2001, p. 104). Like the P21 framework, Confucius is of the view that learning should not lead to theoretical knowledge for its own sake, but knowledge that should actively be used.

Furthermore, Confucian philosophy resonates with Trilling and Fadel's (2009) argument that 'recent research in cognition' has 'punctured a time-honored tenet of teaching–that mastering content must come before an attempt to put it to good use'. On the contrary, 'using knowledge as it is being learned–applying skills like critical thinking, problem solving, and creativity to the content knowledge–increases motivation and improves learning outcomes' (p. 50). In the Confucian tradition, no strict dichotomy exists between mastery of content and the application of this content. As evident in the *Daxue*, learning and its application through active doing is an interrelated, dynamic process whereby one constantly morphs into the other (Chan, 1963). Just as learning enables one to apply and actively put it into practice, active doing as one learns facilitates learning.

It is clear therefore, that all three aspects of critical thinking noted by Trilling and Fadel resonate with Confucian philosophy. To recapitulate, for both Confucius and the P21 framework, critical thinking cannot take place in a vacuum without the acquisition of a knowledge core. Additionally, it is crucial for critical thinkers to ask questions. Contrary to Bloom's taxonomy, learners ought to engage in complex thinking, such as the synthesis of knowledge, in a holistic, non-hierarchical manner, and actively apply knowledge as it is being learned. Clearly, the P21 framework resists the tendency to construe learning in an atomistic, linear fashion, one that moves rigidly from 'lower-level' to 'higher-order' thinking skills and from learning to active application. Its emphasis on a more holistic, 'all-at-once' approach finds weight in the philosophical tradition of Confucianism.

Notwithstanding the similarities noted between Confucian ideas and the P21 framework, Confucian philosophy also provides fresh perspectives in the notion that thinking is not a strictly cognitive endeavour, but an affective one as well. In the Confucian tradition, thinking cannot be divorced from feeling. The Chinese character 心 (*xin*) refers to both the 'heart' *and* the 'mind'; the affective cannot be dissociated from the cognitive (Ames, 2003). If this were accepted by mainstream educational theory, the Bloom's taxonomy would not only have to be re-written in a non-linear and non-hierarchical manner, but would also have to include insights from other affective theories and taxonomies as well.

Communication and Collaboration

For Trilling and Fadel (2009), communication and collaboration skills are crucial to promote learning together in the twenty-first century. They argue that while education has traditionally focused on the importance of good communication, such as skills in reading, writing and speaking, the demands of this century and digital technology necessitates 'a much wider and deeper personal portfolio of communication and collaboration skills to promote learning together' (p. 54). This means that learners ought to be able to 'communicate clearly' and 'collaborate with others' (p. 55). In short, they need to learn the skills of 'complex communicating' (p. 49). Teamwork is important, and humans have to work with and relate to one another. As I shall show, the Confucian philosophical enterprise emphasises these values.

With respect to communicating clearly, Trilling and Fadel (2009) stress the need for twenty-first century learners to 'articulate thoughts and ideas effectively using oral, written and nonverbal communication skills in a variety of forms and contexts'. Furthermore, learners ought to be able to 'communicate effectively in diverse environments' and 'use communication for a range of purposes' (p. 55). Clearly, merely learning how to read, write and speak are not enough in the P21 framework. Skills to communicate effectively in complex environments are needed, skills that by no means can easily be taught via traditional book learning.

Confucius may well be the ideal kind of twenty-first century learner that Trilling and Fadel describe. In his home village, he is known to be rather quiet—almost as if he is 'at a loss for words' (*Analects* 10.1; Slingerland, 2003, p. 98). This seeming lack of eloquence is, for Slingerland (2003), 'an expression of reverence' (p. 98) for Confucius' elders; even if he were to disagree with his elders, he would do so in a respectful manner using very few words. However, in the public sphere, such as the ancestral temple and court, he would be articulate with his words (*Analects* 10.1, 3.15, 10.21), though always with caution and restraint. Additionally, at court, Confucius would always be congenial, affable and pleasant to his subordinates, and respectful but straightforward to his superiors (*Analects* 10.2). In short, Confucius adapts his speech, behaviour and countenance according to changing social demands (i.e. between family and public life, and between superiors and subordinates). Clearly, as Trilling and Fadel would argue, Confucius is able to articulate his thoughts and communicate effectively in diverse situations; he goes beyond the three 'r's of reading, writing and arithmetic.

Another aspect of effective communication, for Trilling and Fadel (2009), is the ability to 'listen effectively to decipher meaning, including knowledge, values, attitudes and intentions' (p. 55). The importance of listening cannot be overemphasised in the Confucian tradition. Contra Plato who is pejorative about those who 'rate their ears above their intellect' (The *Republic*, 531b), the Confucian sage is one who listens: the Chinese character for the ear (*er*耳) is embedded in the characters for the sage (*sheng*聖) and intelligence (*cong*聰) (DeWoskin, 1982). Hall and Ames (1987) go so far as to term the Confucian sage a symphony orchestra 'conductor', one who 'conduces to a collaboration of unique contributions' through 'various media of communication and communion', thus fostering 'harmony that at once achieves unity while preserving diversity' (p. 278). Like an orchestral conductor, the Confucian sage, as Trilling and Fadel (2009) would say, 'listens effectively' (p. 55) to the voices of different personalities. Differences are not suppressed, but harmonised in such a way that the whole is greater than the sum of its parts. Just as an orchestral conductor listens carefully to the players to decipher their creative intent (Tan, 2014, 2016), the twenty-first century learner ought to acquire the skill of keen listening in order for genuine communication to happen.

With respect to collaborating with others, Trilling and Fadel (2009) highlight the need for learners to not only 'work effectively and respectfully with diverse teams', but also to 'exercise flexibility and willingness to be helpful in making necessary compromises to accomplish a common goal' (p. 55). These values lie at the core of Confucianism. Confucius explicitly warns against being stubborn and inflexible (*Analects* 9.4), which recalls his doctrine of timeliness (*shi* 時): 'responding flexibly and appropriately to the situation with which one is confronted' (*Analects* 7.11; Slingerland, 2003, p. 67). For Confucius, since every situation in life differs, one should not apply moral rules in a rigid fashion (*Analects* 18.8). Rather, an ethically exemplary person (*junzi*君子) makes the appropriate judgement at the appropriate time. Flexibility that is similarly emphasised by the P21 framework is required.

In fact, one might go a step further to argue that Confucian philosophy is undergirded by assumptions that emphasises the importance of collaboration to an even greater degree than the P21 framework. For Trilling and Fadel (2009), learners ought to 'assume shared responsibility for collaborative work, and value the individual contributions made by each team member' (p. 55). Notwithstanding the emphasis on teamwork, it nonetheless remains rather individualistic in its call to 'value the *individual* contributions made by *each* team member' (emphasis added). The basic point of reference remains the individual: it is individuals who contribute to the collective.

An illustration serves to contrast an individualistic construal of the self against a Confucian construal. Take, for example, two teachers, one in Britain, the other in Taiwan. When addressing their respective classes, the first teacher is likely to use the word 'everyone' (e.g. 'Everyone, please stand up'). The second teacher, speaking in Mandarin, will probably say, '大家' (*dajia*), which does mean 'everyone', but literally translates as 'big family' (i.e. '*Big family*, please stand up') (Ames, 2011, p. 105). While the English language construes 'every*one*' in the class as being a sum total of discrete, singular individuals, the Chinese language portrays all class members as belonging to one 'big family' (*dajia* 大家). This distinction is not trivial. The Western portrait of the self is inextricably linked to the notion of the 'atomic individual' that harks back to the soul of the Greek and Christian traditions. According to this construal, each human being has an internal experience: even if a body is being cut, there nonetheless exists an internal thing—the 'real' self or the 'soul'. By contrast, in the Confucian tradition, there is neither a self nor a soul that is present when a person is born (Ames, 2011, p. 96). Rather, what constitutes a self and personality flows from the community, in particular, the family. One is not born a human *being* with a ready-made soul, but *becomes* human ('human becoming') by fostering relations with the family and community (Ames, 2011, p. 87).

The Confucian portrait of the self, therefore, is irreducibly social and radically relational. One cannot be truly human *in silo*, but only in relation to others. The P21 framework, with its emphasis on 'the *individual* contributions made by *each* team member', sees the individual as a matter of antecedent reality who then contributes to the whole by working with other individuals. With the Confucian framework, it is the collective that comprises the antecedent reality: relationality and interdependence are the basis of departure. This theory of the social self foreshadows that of the American pragmatist George Herbert Mead, who argues that 'the whole (society) is prior to the part (the individual), not the part to the whole; and the part is explained in terms of the whole, not the whole in terms of the part or parts' (Mead, 1934, p. 37). A person is always a part of a larger community, which in turn is a part of an even larger community, and so on. The fingernail is a part of the finger, which in turn is a part of the hand, which in turn is a part of the limbs, and the entire body. The notion of the fingernail in and of itself is meaningless—a holistic construal of the human body that forms the basis of Traditional Chinese Medicine (Ames, 2011).

The importance of communication and collaboration in the Confucian tradition, therefore, is emphasised to an even deeper degree than the P21 framework. Notwithstanding the call for communication and collaboration in many major twenty-first century skills frameworks, Tan (2013) argues that these frameworks are founded on an individualist construal of education as their focus are on the need to enable learners to compete, get ahead of others and succeed in the present globalised world. Tan warns that while there is nothing wrong in this in and of itself, it may possibly 'foster excessive self-centeredness and unhealthy competition rather than peaceful co-existence and altruistic collaboration among people', further noting that 'we should learn to benefit ourselves as well as others since the two cannot be separated–to help ourselves, according to Confucius, is to help others' (p. 4). When one organ of the body functions well, the other organs and the entire body are healthy too.

To summarise, Confucian philosophy buttresses the P21 framework in its emphasis on the need for learners to articulate their thoughts and ideas, being adaptable to diverse environments, listening effectively, and exercising flexibility when working in teams. In its construal of humans as being inextricably linked to others, it offers an alternative pair of lenses from which to view collaboration—one that does not construe the world in terms of individualistic competition and zero-sum game.

Creativity

For Trilling and Fadel (2009), creativity ranks very highly on the inventory of twenty-first century skills; this is because the world's global economy has a constant demand for new products and services. Despite the general acceptance of creativity worldwide as a good (e.g. Craft, 2003), research has indicated the presence of a stereotypical conception that Asians (and by extension, their education systems) are less creative than people from the West, a view held not just by Westerners, but also Asians themselves (e.g. Niu, 2012; Wong & Niu, 2012). In *Why Asians are less creative* (Ng, 2001), Singaporean writer Ng Aik Kwang attributes the supposed lack of creativity to the Confucian tradition. After all, Confucius said that 'I transmit rather than innovate. I trust in and love the ancient ways' (*Analects* 7.1; Slingerland, 2003, p. 64). Is the pursuit of creativity in the P21 framework then, fundamentally at odds with Confucian philosophy? In the discussion that ensues, I argue that Confucian philosophy not only resonates with key ideas on creativity in the P21 framework, but also has much to nuance and enhance it. Indeed, as Wen (2009) argues, there are dimensions of Confucian philosophy that are 'profoundly creative' (p. 1).

For Trilling and Fadel (2009), a learning environment that nurtures creativity is one that fosters 'questioning, patience, openness to fresh ideas', and 'high levels of trust' (pp. 57–58). All four aspects can also be seen in the Confucian tradition. First, a learning environment that emphasises questioning is important to Confucius. Speaking of his disciple Yan Hui, Confucius notes how 'I can talk all day long with Yan Hui without him once disagreeing with me. In this way, he seems a bit stupid' (*Analects* 2.9; Slingerland, 2003, p. 11). Clearly, Confucius expects his students to question him. Additionally, Confucius models the art of questioning in his own teaching—the *Analects* is filled with conversations between Confucius and his students, many of which feature the master questioning his students. In the artful use of questions in teaching, Confucius' approach recalls that of Socrates, which has a similar maieutic quality (Slingerland, 2003; Tan, 2014). Second, patience is emphasised in the Confucian learning environment. The *Analects*—arguably the most important document of Confucius' teachings—opens with Confucius stressing the importance of devoting oneself to long periods of study, even when one's talents are not recognised (*Analects* 1.1). For Confucius, one should not seek immediate rewards and recognition, but ought to study for its own sake. Confucius models such patience in teaching and learning, and is known as someone who teaches others 'without growing weary' (*Analects* 7.2; Ames & Rosement, 1998, p. 111). Third, Confucius' 'openness to fresh ideas' (Trilling & Fadel, 2009, p. 57) can be seen in how he listens to and learns from the people around him, and selects what is good and follows it (*Analects* 7.28). He also explicitly forbids being stubborn, demanding absolute certainty, and insisting on oneself (*Analects* 9.4). Fourth, Trilling and Fadel's (2009) emphasis on 'high levels of trust' finds resonance in the Confucian philosophical tradition where trust or *xin* (信) is one of the six desirable character traits (*Analects* 17.8). In fact, Confucius goes so far as to teach his disciples to 'let your actions be governed by dutifulness and trust-worthiness *xin* (信), and do not accept as a friend one who is not your equal' in this regard (*Analects* 9.25; Slingerland, 2003, p. 95).

Trilling and Fadel's call for educators to create environments that nurture creativity betrays an underlying assumption of the P21 framework: the notion that creativity is something that can be developed. For Trilling and Fadel (2009), it is a common misconception that 'creativity is only for geniuses' (p. 57). In so doing, they seek to overturn a notion of the creative genius seen most clearly in the writings of Continental philosophers such as Schopenhauer (2011), who argues that genuine art is produced by those who have been 'inspired to the point of genius' (p. 261), and Kant (2000), who posits that 'beautiful art is art of genius' (p. 186). Trilling and Fadel's efforts to dispel the Western notion of genius resonates with the Confucian tradition, where no such notion of genius exists. Contra Western *creatio ex nihilo* where creativity is construed in terms of the Judeo-Christian God's transcendent act of 'creating from nothing' (and hence requires genius), Confucian creativity—*creatio in situ* or 'situational creativity'—renders creativity in terms of flexible responses to ever-changing situations (Ames, 2005; Hall & Ames, 1987; Niu & Sternberg, 2006; Tan, 2016; Wen, 2009). Like the P21 framework, Confucian philosophy is of the view that creativity can be developed, thus providing an alternative philosophical resource on which Trilling and Fadel's arguments may lean on.

Furthermore, Trilling and Fadel's critique of the individual creative genius also implies that creativity does not necessarily have to be construed in individualistic terms; rather, it is important for learners to collaborate with others. Such a notion of creativity resonates with Confucian creativity. Unlike Western *creatio ex nihilo* that dichotomises the Creator and the created, Confucian *creatio in situ* construes humans as co-creators of the cosmos. While *tian* (天: heaven/sky) creates, it is humans who continue *tian*'s work to extend the *dao* (道) or the Way (*Analects* 15.29; Ames & Rosemont, 1998; Ames & Hall, 2001). In the classical Confucian worldview, humans collaborate with *tian* to create the world; the universe is by no means solely created by a single God. It follows therefore, that a collaborative view of creativity lies at the heart of Confucian *creatio in situ*. In fact, just as the Confucian view of the self is irreducibly social and stresses interdependence, the Confucian notion of creativity is collaborative right from the outset: *tian* and humans *require* one another; creativity cannot be achieved without one or the other. No one ever creates alone; the others matter. And because the others matter, what one creates is inextricably linked to the larger socio-cultural context. Although novelty is prized, appropriateness or *yi* (義) is valued in Confucian creativity as well (Niu, 2012); creativity is not so much for its own sake as it is to be of value to society. This resonates with Trilling and Fadel's (2009) comment that 'students must invent solutions to real-world problems' (p. 58). Contra

Oscar Wilde's 'art for art's sake' which has roots in Kantian philosophy (e.g. Kant, 2000), the practical value of creativity is crucial for both Confucius and the P21 framework.

In short, Confucian philosophy provides theoretical foundation for the P21 framework in terms of the ideal learning environment to foster creativity, the notion that creativity can be nurtured, the nullification of the solitary creative genius, and the proposition of a collaborative and practical construal of creativity. It must be stressed, however, that in its emphasis on the practical value of creativity, Confucian philosophy, unlike the P21 framework, is not driven by economic concerns, but by a desire to meliorate the world in which we live. For Trilling and Fadel (2009), the purpose of engaging in collaborative creativity with others is ultimately to lead to 'useful real-world innovations, a prize skill in our twenty-first century innovation-driven economy' (p. 58). For Confucius, however, creativity is an ethical endeavour (Tan, 2015). As noted by several prominent Confucian scholars, such as Tu Weiming and Roger Ames, *cheng* (誠)—often translated as 'sincerity'—is inextricably linked to creativity (Ames & Hall, 2001; Tan, 2016; Tu, 1989). So important is *cheng* to creativity that according to the *Zhongyong*, '*cheng* is the beginning and end of things', further noting that 'without *cheng*, there would be nothing' (Chan, 1963, p. 108). In addition to sincerity, *cheng* may also refer to 'perfect genuineness', 'authenticity', 'integrity', 'to complete' and 'to perfect' (Ames & Hall, 2001, p. 33; Tan, 2012, p. 134). Clearly, creativity is construed in the Confucian tradition not as a means of being competitive and getting ahead of others, but to create a better world through the many virtues and values encapsulated by the single character, *cheng* (誠).

Conclusion

This article was prompted by two questions posed in the opening paragraph: How do the twenty-first century skills resonate with Confucian ideas? How might Confucian philosophy contribute to a twenty-first century approach to education in this present globalised world? It is hopefully clear from this article that there are indeed ideas in the P21 framework that resonate with Confucian philosophy and are relevant to Confucian-heritage societies. Furthermore, Confucian philosophy contributes to a twenty-first century approach to education by adding nuance to the existing P21 framework. As noted in the discussion above, these include the notion that critical thinking is not a strictly cognitive endeavour but an affective one as well, a social and relational construal of the human self, and an ethical notion of creativity. The significance of this discussion and comparison lies in these three key aspects in which Confucian philosophy might contribute to P21 globally.

This article also raises deeper questions for global education. For example, notwithstanding the influence of classical Confucianism over huge stretches of Asia, including Mainland China, Taiwan, Japan, Korea, Vietnam and Singapore (Tu, 1996), this article cannot claim to speak for all of Asian philosophy as it draws on only three Confucian texts. Indeed, it remains to be seen how other Asian philosophical traditions—such as Indian, Islamic and Thai philosophies—may compare with, add value, or even clash with extant twenty-first century frameworks. This article is further limited in the omission of other philosophical schools in classical China, later developments in Confucianism, and other twenty-first century skills frameworks. How would the P21 framework look like if it were to synthesise insights from myriad philosophical traditions? Is a genuinely global and transcultural approach to twenty-first century education possible? These questions remain to be answered. Nonetheless, other writers may build on my work for further research, and I hope to have contributed to philosophical dialogue between Asia and the West. Surely, this is much needed for the globalised world of the twenty-first century.

Disclosure statement

No potential conflict of interest was reported by the author.

ORCID

Leonard Tan http://orcid.org/0000-0003-3514-8315

References

Ames, R. (2003). Confucianism and Deweyan pragmatism. *Journal of Chinese Philosophy, 30,* 403–417.
Ames, R. (2005). Collaterality in early Chinese cosmology: An argument for Confucian harmony (*he* 和) as *creatio in situ*. *Taiwan Journal of East Asian Studies, 2,* 43–70.
Ames, R. (2011). *Confucian role ethics: A vocabulary*. Honolulu: University of Hawaii Press.
Ames, R., & Hall, D. (2001). *Focusing the familiar – A translation and philosophical interpretation of the Zhongyong*. Honolulu: University of Hawaii Press.
Ames, R., & Rosement, H. (1998). *The Analects of Confucius: A philosophical translation*. New York, NY: Ballantine Publishing Group.
Ananiadou, K., & Claro, M. (2009). *21st century skills and competences for new millennium learners in OECD countries* (Education Working Paper No. 41). Paris: Organization for Economic Co-operation and Development. Retrieved from http://www.oecd.org/officialdocuments/publicdisplaydocumentpdf/?cote=EDU/WKP%282009%2920&doclanguage=en
Binkley, M., Erstad, O., Herman, J., Raizen, S., Ripley, M., Miller-Ricci, M., & Rumble, M. (2012). Defining twenty-first century skills. In P. Griffin, B. McGaw, & E. Care (Eds.), *Assessment and teaching of 21st century skills* (pp. 17–66). Dordrecht: Springer.
Chan, W. (1963). *A source book in Chinese philosophy*. Princeton, NJ: Princeton University Press.
Craft, A. (2003). The limits to creativity in education: Dilemmas for the educator. *British Journal of Educational Studies, 51,* 113–127. doi:10.1111/1467-8527.t01-1-00229
European Parliament and the Council of the European Union. (2007). *Key competences for lifelong learning: European reference framework*. Luxembourg City: Office for Official Publications of the European Communities. Retrieved from http://www.alfa-trall.eu/wp-content/uploads/2012/01/EU2007-keyCompetencesL3-brochure.pdf

Hall, D., & Ames, R. (1987). *Thinking through Confucius*. Albany, NY: State University of New York Press.
Kant, I. (2000). *Critique of the power of judgment* (P. Guyer & E. Matthews, Trans.). New York, NY: Cambridge University Press. (Original work published 1790)
Kim, H. K. (2003). Critical thinking, learning and Confucius: A positive assessment. *Journal of philosophy of education, 37,* 71–87.
Mead, G. H. (1934). *Mind, self and society from the standpoint of a social behaviorist*. Chicago, IL: The University of Chicago Press.
National Research Council (2012). *Education for life and work: Developing transferable knowledge and skills in the 21st century*. Washington, DC: National Academies Press.
Ng, A. K. (2001). *Why Asians are less creative than Westerners*. Singapore: Prentice Hall.
Niu, W. (2012). Confucian ideology and creativity. *The Journal of Creative Behavior, 46,* 274–284. doi:10.1002/jocb.18
Niu, W., & Sternberg, R. J. (2006). The philosophical roots of Western and Eastern conceptions of creativity. *Journal of Theoretical & Philosophical Psychology, 26,* 18–38. doi:10.1037/h0091265
Partnership for 21st Century Skills. (2009a). *Framework for 21st century learning*. Washington, DC: Author. Retrieved from http://www.p21.org/our-work/p21-framework
Partnership for 21st Century Skills. (2009b). *P21 framework definitions*. Washington, DC: Author. Retrieved from www.p21.org/storage/documents/P21_Framework_Definitions.pdf
Resnick, L. B., & Hall, M. W. (1998). Learning organizations for sustainable education reform. *Daedalus, 127,* 89–118.
Schopenhauer, A.. (2011). The world as will and representation (3rd ed). In J. Norman, A. Welchman, and C. Janaway(Eds.), *The cambridge edition of the works of Schopenhauer*, vol. 1 (pp. 23–440). Cambridge: Cambridge University Press. (Original work published 1818)
Slingerland, E. (2003). *Confucius Analects – With selections from traditional commentaries*. Indianapolis, IN: Hackett Publishing Company.
Starr, D. (2012). China and the Confucian education model. *Universitas, 21,* 1–27.
Tan, L. (2012). *Towards a transcultural philosophy of instrumental music education* (Unpublished doctoral dissertation). Indiana University.
Tan, C. (2013). A Confucian framework for 21st century education (PLS Working Paper 2). Retrieved from https://plsworkingpapers.files.wordpress.com/2014/03/pls-working-paper-series-no-22.pdf
Tan, L. (2014). Towards a transcultural theory of democracy for instrumental music education. *Philosophy of Music Education Review, 22,* 61–77. doi:10.2979/philmusieducrevi.22.1.61
Tan, C. (2015). Beyond rote-memorisation: Confucius' concept of thinking. *Educational philosophy and theory: Incorporating ACCESS, 47,* 428–439. doi:10.1080/00131857.2013.879693
Tan, L. (2016). Confucian *creatio in situ* – Philosophical resource for a theory of creativity in instrumental music education. *Music Education Research,* 18 (1), 91–108, doi:10.1080/14613808.2014.993602
Trilling, B., & Fadel, C. (2009). *21st century skills: Learning for life in our times*. San Francisco, CA: Jossey-Bass.
Tu, W. M. (1989). *Centrality and commonality – An essay on Confucian religiousness*. Albany, NY: State University of New York Press.
Tu, W. M. (1996). *Confucian traditions in East Asian modernity – Moral education and economic culture in Japan and the four mini-dragons*. Cambridge, MA: Harvard University Press.
Voogt, J., & Roblin, N. P. (2012). A comparative analysis of international frameworks for 21st century competences: Implications for national curriculum policies. *Journal of Curriculum Studies, 44,* 299–321. doi:10.1080/00220272.2012.668938
Wen, H. (2009). *Confucian pragmatism as the art of contextualizing personal experience and world*. Lanham: Lexington Books.
Wong, R., & Niu, W. (2012). Cultural difference in stereotype perceptions and performances in non-verbal deductive reasoning and creativity. *Journal of Creative Behavior, 46,* 345–363.

Problem-Centered Design and Personal Teaching Style: An exploratory study of Youguang Tu's course on philosophy of education

HONGDE LEI

Abstract

Youguang Tu is a contemporary Chinese philosopher of education. His course on philosophy of education had a significant impact on his students. This exploratory study examines how Tu designed and taught this course. Ultimately, there are two reasons why Tu's course had such a significant influence on his students. The first is that Tu used problem-centered design to address both central problems of education and specific problems that students encountered. The second is that Tu exhibited a personal teaching style that incorporated elegant handwriting, appropriate analogies, and fierce passion.

Introduction

As a contemporary Chinese philosopher of education, Youguang Tu (1927–2012) has attracted increasing attention in academic circles (Luo, 2015; Zuo & Lei, 2015). In his youth, under the guidance of his father, he thoroughly familiarized himself with Chinese traditional classics such as the Confucian *Analects*, the *Mengzi*, *Gang Jian Lüe*, and *Qian Jia Shi*, laying a sturdy and solid foundation that he would draw on throughout his life. In 1948, after testing into Tsinghua University's Philosophy Department, Tu and famous Chinese philosopher Youlan Feng built a close relationship that lasted more than forty years. According to classmates and colleagues, the enduring, intimate nature of this intellectual partnership enabled Tu to understand Feng's philosophy 'perhaps better than anyone' (Obenchain, 1994, p. xxxvi). As a result, he was widely known as Feng's 'Number One Student'. After the Cultural Revolution (1966–1976) had passed, Tu translated Feng's works, transcribed Feng's

A KALEIDOSCOPIC VIEW OF CHINESE PHILOSOPHY OF EDUCATION

Oral Autobiography at the Hall of the Three Pines (*Sansongtang Zixu*, 三松堂自序), and involved himself in the discussion and writing of Feng's final work, *A History of Chinese Philosophy (New Edition)*. In addition, Tu spent ten years independently compiling and editing the 14-volume *Collected Works at the Hall of Three Pines* (*Sansongtang Quanji*,三松堂全集), the length of which ultimately reached up to four million Chinese characters. Tu's work rejuvenated 'Feng Studies' (which had been disparaged during the Cultural Revolution), and reconstructed Feng's academic image.

By 1993, Tu had produced fruitful research on Youlan Feng, philosophy of China's ancient Chu Kingdom, and Chinese traditional culture. In 1993, he was brought out of retirement by the School of Education at Huazhong University of Science and Technology. Thereafter, he devoted himself to researching the history of Chinese higher education and other fundamental aspects of education. The legacy of Tu's educational research is concentrated in 'one book and one course' (Lei, 2010). The 'book' refers to his monograph, *A Critical History of Chinese Higher Education*, while the 'course' indicates his class on the philosophy of education. Tu taught this course to graduate students every year from 1999 to 2010, and the course accounted for 32 credit hours. For many students, participating in this course constituted an unforgettable experience. As one attests, 'Professor Tu's course stood out from the rest: it frequently shook my spirit to the core' (Zhu, 2004, p. 68). Another states, 'Professor Tu's penetrating insight—derived from reflection and intuition—often allowed students a breath of fresh air, and even furnished lifelong memories' (Wang, 2004, p. 66). One former student even declares, 'The time we spent in that course was limited, but the extent to which students were transformed by Tu's magnificent demeanor, personal teaching style, and educational thought is limitless' (Liu, 2004, pp. 65, 66).

The volume and intensity of such feedback demonstrates that Tu's course on philosophy of education had a significant impact on his students. How might this impact be explained? The aim of this article is to answer this question by exploring how Tu designed and taught his course.

Tu's Problem-Centered Design

Central Problems of Education

The design of Tu's course on philosophy of education was problem-centered, focusing on both central problems of contemporary education and specific problems encountered by students. Tu divided his course content into six parts and addressed only one central problem in each part. In the words of R. Current, he did 'philosophically sound and interesting work on fundamental and controversial aspects of education' (Current, 2010).

The central problem addressed in the first part of Tu's course on the philosophy of education is the scientism that is very popular in contemporary Chinese education. According to a classical definition, 'Scientism is a matter of putting too high a value on natural science in comparison with other branches of learning or culture'

(Sorell, 1994, p. 1). Tu was strongly opposed to scientism, and set a high value on philosophy and its role. In his opinion,

> Philosophy and science are two kinds of knowledge that are closely connected and substantially different in terms of their methods and goals. Philosophy can provide guidance for science, and in turn science can help philosophy avoid emptiness. People can conduct either philosophical or scientific inquiry into any subjects. Philosophical inquiry is conducted mainly by reflection and intuition, and its primary goal is the elevation of the mind; meanwhile, scientific inquiry is conducted mainly by observation and experimentation, and its primary goal is the increase of positive knowledge. (Tu, 2004a)

Given the context of a Chinese education system that regularly touts 'scientific development' as a panacea for social problems, Tu's decision to bring attention to the complementary, mutually necessary relationship between science and philosophy was particularly significant. By placing philosophy and science on equal footing, Tu encouraged students to question socially constructed hierarchies of knowledge presented to them in prior academic settings. Furthermore, Tu's intentional placement of this problem at the beginning of his course set a tone for the course, pushing students to continue thinking critically about epistemology.

The central problem addressed in the second part of Tu's course was the subordination of education to politics and economics. Although society is a holistic entity, for the convenience of analysis, it can be divided into three domains: the political, the economic, and the cultural. Tu labeled the respective cores of these three domains as power, profit, and truth (Tu, 1998). He insisted that education should be placed in the cultural domain, prioritizing the pursuit of truth as its core. However, Tu was sad to find that, historically, education was often misplaced. For example, from 1949 to 1978, China experienced many political movements that subordinated education to political exigencies. The so-called 'Cultural Revolution' was not cultural in essence; it was actually a tumultuous ten-year political movement. Amid calls for class struggle, education was tragically politicized, resulting in an entire generation missing the opportunity to attend school. Similarly, in 1978 China adopted its policy of 'Reform and Opening' and changed its core ideology from class struggle to economic development. Unable to resist this new trend, education was often subsumed under the economic domain. Tu was disgusted by the problems that accompanied the commercialization or industrialization of education. He explicitly argued that the proper domain for education should be culture, and that education should use truth to serve politics and economics while simultaneously receiving political and economic support.

The third part of Tu's problem-centered course covered the unreasonable emphasis on educational resources over true educational quality. In this part, Tu proposed a new concept called 'education itself' that was defined as follows: 'Education itself is a cultural activity, in which human nature including knowing, feeling, and willing develops intellectually, morally, and physically' (Tu, 2004b). He clearly distinguished developing 'education itself' from improving 'educational conditions' such as schools, campus buildings, and research facilities:

A KALEIDOSCOPIC VIEW OF CHINESE PHILOSOPHY OF EDUCATION

> Education itself and educational conditions merely have a potential connection that is by no means an inevitable relationship. For example, a school is a part of educational conditions, if it is well managed, it can develop education itself. However, if it is not well managed, it can be detrimental to education itself. Comparatively speaking, education itself is internal, and educational conditions are external. It is more difficult to improve education itself, and it takes a longer time for improvements in education itself to appear. Educational conditions are precisely the opposite. (Tu, 2004b)

Tu was disappointed to find that many educational leaders and administrators invested more resources in improving educational conditions because they wanted to make their achievements emerge faster and seem more significant. In the process of pursuing such achievements, education itself is often neglected. In view of this problem, Tu strongly appealed for the reasonable use of educational resources, and highly recommended giving education itself priority over educational conditions.

The fourth central problem featured in Tu's course was the lack of emphasis on practical knowledge for modern learners. According to Tu, knowledge can be categorized as either verbal or practical. Contemporary Chinese education generally emphasizes rote learning—a form of verbal knowledge that helps learners get high scores on exams. However, learners often graduate with very limited practical knowledge. Although a lack of verbal knowledge is unacceptable, to merely be satisfied with verbal knowledge is even more unacceptable. In other words, learners should strive to enter a stage of learning in which they obtain practical knowledge. When knowledge is joined with practice, practice becomes a carrier of knowledge. In order to help learners become better prepared for the job market and real life, Tu clearly suggested that contemporary Chinese education should place more emphasis on practical knowledge.

Tu's fifth central problem concerned the lack of emphasis placed on encouraging students to ruminate over what they learn. This part focused on the methodology of education, and addressed the fundamental aspects concerning what Tu termed the 'principle of experience' and the 'principle of rumination'. The 'principle of experience' means that learners should increase their experience and value learning based on experience. The 'principle of rumination' means that learners should first 'digest' the cultural classics—even though they do not understand them when they are young —and then 'ruminate' to understand and apply what they 'digest' as they grow up. The philosophy of experience, developed carefully by John Dewey, is closely related to education (Dewey, 1938). Primarily drawing from Dewey's ideas, Tu invented the term 'principle of experience' to stress the importance of experience in education. In his opinion, Western countries, especially America, have made great achievements in education by following the 'principle of experience'. Meanwhile, China has successfully enabled cultural continuity for thousands of years by following the 'principle of rumination'. More than a century after the Opium War in 1840, China has gradually accepted and applied the 'principle of experience' in its education by opening up to and learning from Western countries. This is a welcome change. However, it is important to note that the 'principle of rumination' has basically been ignored in

Chinese contemporary education so that most students know very little of their cultural classics. As a consequence, the continuity of various aspects of Chinese culture faces serious challenges. In order to address this problem, Tu suggested reapplying the 'principle of rumination' and combining it with the 'principle of experience'. In his opinion, only if the two principles are applied together will we find perfect educational methods.

The central problem addressed in the sixth and final part of Tu's course was the incomplete nature of the educative process. Contemporary Chinese education is deeply affected by intellectualism that treats knowledge transfer and intellectual pursuit as its primary goals. Tu was not opposed to knowledge transfer and intellectual pursuit; however, he firmly believed it is not enough for education to transfer knowledge and to make human beings intelligent. He stated that:

> Before receiving education, human beings are ignorant, requiring education in order to gain knowledge and become intelligent. However, human beings should continue to receive education in order to be ignorant again. This complete educative process can be expressed in the formula 'ignorant$_1$ → intelligent → ignorant$_2$'. The formula contains two 'ignorant': the first one is original and a gift of nature; the second one is acquired and the creation of spirit. (Tu, 2004c)

According to the above passage, a complete education process includes two stages. The first stage is 'ignorant$_1$ → intelligent', which is mainly a process of cognitive development. The second stage is 'intelligent → ignorant$_2$', which is mainly a process of moral development. An ignorant$_2$ human being is not without intelligence, but he/she does not misuse intelligence for personal gain. It is very dangerous if the educative process is only 'ignorant$_1$ → intelligent'. Without the process of 'intelligent → ignorant$_2$'—in other words, without moral development—an intelligent human being can cause greater harm to others than those who are ignorant.

Specific Problems Encountered by Students

When designing a course, not only is it necessary to prepare course content, but one must also understand the students taking the course, or else one is merely shooting without aim. Tu understood this point: he actively observed his students, and also liked to converse with them. He had considerable contact with students and accepted nearly all those who came seeking his advice. During this process, he discovered that the students he taught shared several problems in common, and therefore prepared his classes to address these problems. While teaching, he would monitor students' responses, and would accordingly revise his pedagogy. He used a formula, '$w = i + r$', (Tu, 2009, p. 303) to describe his pedagogy: 'w' represents his words, 'i' represents his ideas, and 'r' represents the students' responses. His approach to pedagogy was not one of saying whatever came to his mind, but instead, one of joining what he wished to communicate with how students would respond. In this process, he specifically tailored his pedagogy to problems commonly faced by students.

A KALEIDOSCOPIC VIEW OF CHINESE PHILOSOPHY OF EDUCATION

Today, many students dislike reading the classics and original texts. They pay attention to hot topics and ignore fundamental aspects; they are accustomed to using the words of others and lack the habit of self-reflection. Tu was very concerned with the above problems, and adapted a few specific measures in response. For instance, the reading materials he recommended or supplied in his course on philosophy of education were all either classics or original texts. He believed that knowledge had no so-called differentiation between 'hot' and 'cold', insisting that a course on philosophy of education must be dedicated to exploring the fundamental aspects of education. He also strongly believed that, in terms of studying philosophy of education, one's own 'life book' is most worth reading—a task accomplished through reflection.

Through prolonged observation and exchange, Tu realized that, with regard to cognition and comprehension, students possess a considerable amount of knowledge, but their understanding of that knowledge is rather shallow. In terms of scientific and philosophical thought, their scientific thought is relatively well developed, while their philosophical thought is conspicuously lacking. With regard to Chinese and Western learning, today's Chinese students are more interested in Western learning, and often consider Chinese classics to be dull. Many even have misunderstandings and biases when it comes to their own culture. Facing these challenges, Tu consciously tailored his course as follows:

> I lecture more about Chinese learning and philosophical thought, using history as content and literature as form. Moreover, I link and compare Chinese and English, the past and the present, and center my teaching to facilitate deep understanding. (Tu, 2009, p. 303)

Tu's Personal Teaching Style

Elegant Blackboard Calligraphy

Whenever Tu lectured, he always used the blackboard. When he started teaching his course on philosophy of education, his class was not located in a classroom, but in his research room. Since the walls there did not have a blackboard, he simply prepared a five-meter-long, one-meter-wide makeshift blackboard, upon which he did his work. Later on, his teaching location was moved to a classroom equipped with new technologies, but he never used them to teach. In his view, even though the blackboard is an old technology, it is not outdated: it is the most readily available visual aid that could help him achieve his course objectives. For this reason, Tu considered it a waste of time to learn how to use new technologies at that time. Moreover, he firmly believed that penmanship is an important expression of scholarly attainment. In view of the fact that increasingly more students use keyboards to type characters instead of writing them, student penmanship has begun to look progressively less like that of intellectuals. Tu tried to curb this trend by emphasizing the importance of handwriting.

Blackboard writing is both a pedagogic technique and a calligraphic art form. In China, there is a revered tradition in normal university education: namely, stressing training in three forms of handwriting (brush, pen, and chalk). Tu had never received normal education, but his three forms were all very well written. When it came to calligraphy, he possessed an innate artistic ability and practiced assiduously. At five years of age, he began to learn calligraphy, practicing seal script, regular script, running script, and cursive script, with cursive as his forte. At six, he started writing cursive scrolls for people, and was praised as a wunderkind. As he grew older, he never abandoned brush and ink stone, creating many calligraphic works and forming his own style of handwriting. Drawing upon this foundation, he demonstrated nimble, masterful handwriting when writing on the blackboard in class.

It is important to note that despite Tu's particularly beautiful cursive form, he rarely wrote in cursive when teaching, instead relying on running script due to its efficient, recognizable form. He also rarely wrote long sentences or large paragraphs on the board; usually, he would only write classical quotations or central concepts. When writing on the blackboard—especially when writing new or difficult terms—he would often write Chinese and English side by side for comparative purposes. His English handwriting was also very good, tempered through diligent practice. He began learning English in middle school, using a brush to write letters—often times only one per page. In the summer of 1996, he traveled to America to partake in the ninth Conference of the International Society for Chinese Philosophy, where he submitted a handwritten paper in English that was praised by many scholars for its graceful penmanship.

Appropriate Analogies

Tu's scholarship is rooted in philosophy, and the academic world first and foremost recognizes him for his philosophical research. When speaking of philosophy, people almost instinctively associate it with abstraction, generalization, and speculation. Indeed, philosophy has these characteristics, and Tu's philosophy of education is no exception. For instance, the concepts he put forth such as education itself, knowledge itself, original ignorance, and acquired ignorance are indeed abstract, general, and speculative. What sets Tu apart from other educational philosophers, however, is that his philosophy of education has another side to it: namely, it is specific, divergent, and imaginative. These aspects of Tu's philosophy were exhibited in unique pedagogical characteristics, among which there was a trove of appropriate analogies that helped students intuitively grasp complex concepts.

Analogies and definitions are two different ways of speaking. The former states 'this thing resembles something', which results from imaginative thinking; the latter declares 'this thing is something' (Sun, 2010, p. 3), which results from conceptual thinking. Definition is comparable to painting a picture stroke by stroke. Starting from scratch, one must construct a specific concept word by word, element by element, with the ultimate goal of producing a comprehensible unit of meaning. No matter how carefully one 'paints' his/her final concept, the approach is still indirect, and it is still difficult to comprehensively render what you wish to represent. Analogy, however, is not like this. It rather resembles a camera: a click of the shutter, and the object of representation is directly placed within a familiar, comprehensible framework. Definitions require the use of concepts that are often abstract and difficult to understand.

Making up for the inadequacies of definitions, analogies employ concrete images that are easy to understand, but difficult to choose effectively. Drawing an appropriate analogy requires broad knowledge and experience, and demands an aptitude for association—'the ability to join what is present with what is absent, what is manifested with what is hidden, and to find commonalities and intrinsic connections' (Zhang, 2002, p. 49). This is an important teaching skill, and constitutes a trick that excellent teachers like Tu frequently carry up their sleeves.

In 2011, a Chinese American scholar once paid a visit to Tu and asked: If he could only read one book, what would it be? Tu responded without hesitation: the *Zhuangzi*. Throughout his life, Tu ardently loved reading the *Zhuangzi*, digesting and absorbing Master Zhuang's facility for comparison. This led him to use a great deal of fitting analogies—both creative and inspiring—while teaching his course on philosophy of education. For example, when teaching the ontology of education, Tu emphasized that education itself should aim to develop human nature, and that the fundamental content of human nature includes knowing, feeling, and willing. He believed that as components of human nature, the way that these three categories relate to each other is comparable to a car's steering wheel, motor, and driver: the steering wheel represents knowing, the motor represents feeling, and the driver represents willing. Once the motor is started, there is power. This power is controlled by the steering wheel, and the steering wheel is controlled in turn by the driver. If one wishes to drive a car well, one must effectively manage the relationship between the motor, steering wheel, and driver. Similarly, if one wishes to develop human nature well, one must effectively manage the relationship between knowing, feeling, and willing.

Another example of Tu's appropriate analogizing lies in the way he taught the epistemology of education. When teaching epistemology, he proposed the paired concepts of 'knowledge itself' and 'carriers of knowledge'. He declared that knowledge itself is like the shoes people wear, whereas carriers of knowledge are like the footprints that those wearing shoes leave behind. Footprints are left behind by shoes, but they are not the shoes themselves. Moreover, while teaching the methodology of education, Tu put forth his own term 'principle of rumination' and used it to summarize several thousand years of ancient Chinese experience in teaching and learning: first, let students swallow classic literature just as cows swallow grass, then let them ruminate—spit up what was previously eaten, chew slowly, digest, and absorb.

Fierce Passion

Several years ago, I was attracted by the two words 'fierce passion' (Hong, 2008, p. 25) in an article. When I first read these words, Tu immediately came to mind. He was always serious, carrying a solemn expression on his face, wearing neat and plain clothing, and holding perfectly straight posture. He was also full of passion, lecturing vehemently, and sometimes even working himself into a fury. When he would lose his temper, he became all the more revered. Almost all of Tu's students at some point witnessed him lose his temper, and I was no exception.

A KALEIDOSCOPIC VIEW OF CHINESE PHILOSOPHY OF EDUCATION

On 17 September 1997, as a graduate student, I attended my first class at Huazhong University of Science and Technology. When it came time for class to begin, the teacher had not yet arrived. The students at first thought this a bit strange, then soon enough began to chat. After about ten minutes, an elderly man walked into the room. He walked two laps around the classroom, then lightly sat on the wooden chair behind the lectern. We stopped our chatter and waited for him to speak. Who would have thought it—the elderly man sat there, not moving an inch, staring fixedly at us. Suddenly, slapping the table, he rose to his feet and bellowed:

> Lords! Ladies! You've tested into graduate school, and now you think you are *extraordinary*? Learning is sought! It is not something I feed you! If I don't show up, do you not know how to study by yourselves? If I don't lecture, do you not know how to learn? True learning is sought by yourselves—it is not something that I deliver to you. According to Chinese tradition, the superior man advances in what his learning with deep earnestness and by the proper course, wishing to get hold of it by himself. Having got hold of it by himself, he abides in it calmly and firmly. Abiding in it calmly and firmly, he reposes in a deep reliance on it. Reposing in a deep reliance on it, he seizes it on the left and right, meeting everywhere with it as a fountain from which things flow. (Lei, 2004, p. 4)

The roar that the elderly man unleashed lasted about one minute. Afterward, he wrote a big character for 'seek' (*qiu* 求) on the blackboard. Honing in on this character, he excitedly lectured for half an hour. At that time, my classmates and I were all scared into place, simply stupefied. Afterward, we learned that this howler was Tu. At that time he was already 70 years old, and in that first class he gave us all a knock on the head. This knock was just like the rap on the head spoken of in Buddhism, and it produced a shock that continues to reverberate within me to this day.

A research study based on 25 years of examining instruction methods in classrooms discovered, 'A teacher who is excited about the subject being taught and shows it by facial expression, voice inflection, gesture, and general movement is more likely to hold the attention of students than one who does not exhibit these behaviors' (Borich, 2000, p. 25). This type of excitement was evident in Tu's course—his anger was often a product of impulse. Most of the things that made him angry were related to traditional Chinese culture. He had profound affection for traditional culture, as well as the utmost worry for its current state of affairs. Upon encountering students' ignorance, prejudice, or misunderstanding of traditional Chinese culture, he would easily lose his temper. Every time he got angry, he would lose a bit of strength, and would sometimes even fall sick. On the afternoon of 1 April 2010, a student's resistance to his demand for handwritten homework got him worked up, and on the road home he suddenly suffered a stroke caused by high blood pressure. After this, he never again returned to the classroom. Sadly, his course on philosophy of education subsequently ceased to continue.

Conclusion

This exploratory study finds two reasons why Tu's course on philosophy of education had a significant impact on his students. One reason is that Tu used problem-centered design to address the central problems of education and specific problems that students encountered. This type of design had a dual emphasis on both content and students. As famous educational researcher Allan C. Ornstein once explained, 'What makes the design unique is that the content is organized in ways that allow students to clearly view problem areas' (Ornstein & Hunkins, 2010, p. 204). Although some scholars criticize this approach, asserting that students do not learn much subject matter from a course with problem-centered design, Tu insisted that this design facilitated precisely what a truly comprehensive, meaningful education must demand. He steadfastly believed that the content of a course on philosophy of education must be minimized to the essential: a prompt to provoke students' active engagement was sufficient (Luo, 2015). What he stressed most was not how much subject matter students learned, but how well students linked subject matter to the real problems of education and themselves.

Another reason that Tu's philosophy of education course had such a significant influence on his students was that Tu made use of his unique personal teaching style. His elegant blackboard calligraphy made his teaching pleasing to students' eyes; his appropriate analogies explained the profound in simple terms; his fierce passion filled his teaching with the heat of life. He consciously developed his personal teaching style upon the foundation of his innate character. More importantly, he had the courage to use his personal teaching style to break away from redundant or monotonous routines. Bringing personality to teaching is one thing; being able to use it effectively is another. Even if teachers possess their own personal teaching styles, it does not mean that they will be willing or able to use them practically. In China in particular, mainstream traditional culture stresses uniformity and belittles independence. This relentless pressure to conform with one's surroundings often leads to an excessive restriction of divergent thinking. Today, educational standards are growing ever more numerous in Chinese schools, pushing a stultifying uniformity upon teachers and students alike. Under such circumstances, it is becoming increasingly difficult for teachers to develop and draw upon their personal teaching styles. In the twenty-first century in which diversity and innovation are more important than ever, China's Government and educational institutions would do well to learn from the legacy of Tu, not only providing teachers the support necessary to teach content, but the freedom and flexibility required to ignite imaginations anew, using personal strengths to challenge and inspire the minds of all.

Disclosure statement

No potential conflict of interest was reported by the author.

Funding

This research was sponsored by Humanities and Social Sciences Foundation of Ministry of Education of China [project number 14YJA880029].

ORCID

Hongde Lei http://orcid.org/0000-0003-0860-2965

References

Borich, G. D. (2000). *Effective teaching methods* (4th ed.). New Jersey, NJ: Prentice-Hall Inc.

Current, R. (2010). Philosophy of education: Its current trajectories and challenges. In M. Peters, P. Ghiraldelli, B. Žarnić, & A. Gibbons (Eds.), *Encyclopaedia of philosophy of education*. Retrieved from http://www.ffst.hr/ENCYCLOPAEDIA

Dewey, J. (1938). *Experience and education*. New York, NY: Kappa Delta Pi.

Hong, Z. C. (2008). Zai Buqueding zhong Xunzhao Weizhi: Wo de YueduShi zhi Dai Jinhua 在不确定中寻找位置:"我的阅读史"之戴锦华 [Searching for a place amid uncertainty: 'My reading history' of Dai Jinhua]. Wenyi Zhengming 文艺争鸣 [*Arts and Literature Contend*], *22*, 22–28.

Lei, H. D. (2004, October 25). Shi Hou 师吼 [The howl of a teacher]. *Huazhong Keji Daxue Zhoubao* 华中科技大学周报 [*Huazhong University of science and technology weekly*], 4.

Lei, H. D. (2010). Tu Youguang Xiansheng de Daxuezhidao 涂又光先生的大学之道 [On Mr. Youguang Tu's Dao of great learning]. Gaodeng Jiaoyu Yanjiu 高等教育研究 [*Journal of Higher Education*], *31*, 15–21.

Liu, Y. M. (2004). Zuo Zhenren Zhenxuewen de Bangyang 做真人真学问的榜样 [A model of a genuine man and genuine scholarship]. 高等教育研究 [*Journal of Higher Education*], *25*, 65–66.

Luo, H. O. (2015). Zhenzheng de Shizhe 真正的师者：涂又光先生的为师之道 [A real master: Mr. Youguang Tu's Dao of being a teacher]. 教育研究 [*Educational Research*], *36*, 98–104.

Obenchain, D. B. (1994). Feng Youlan's work of a century. *Journal of Chinese Philosophy*, *21*, i–cxii.

Ornstein, A. C., & Hunkins, F. P. (2010). *Curriculum: Foundations, principles, and issues* (5th ed.). Peking: China Renmin University Press.

Sorell, T. (1994). *Scientism: Philosophy and the infatuation with science*. London: Routledge.

Sun, K. Y. (2010). *Jiaoyu Xiangshenme* 教育像什么 [*What does education resemble: A figurative pedagogy*]. 南京，中国：江苏教育出版社 [Nanjing: Jiangsu Education Press].

Tu, Y. G. (1998). Wenming de Bentuhua yu Daxue 文明的本土化与大学 [Indigenization of cultures and universities]. 高等教育研究 [*Journal of Higher Education*], *19*, 5–7.

Tu, Y. G. (2004a). *Jiaoyu Zhexue Diyijiang Ketang Shilu* 教育哲学第一讲课堂实录 [Unabridged record of the first lecture in philosophy of education]. Retrieved from http://wenku.baidu.com

Tu, Y. G. (2004b). *Jiaoyu Zhexue Disanjiang Ketang Shilu* 教育哲学第三讲课堂实录 [Unabridged record of the second lecture in philosophy of education]. Retrieved from http://wenku.baidu.com

Tu, Y. G. (2004c). *Jiaoyu Zhexue Diliujiang Ketang Shilu* 教育哲学第六讲课堂实录 [Unabridged record of the sixth lecture in philosophy of education]. Retrieved from http://wenku.baidu.com

Tu, Y. G. (2009). *Tuyouguang Wencun* 涂又光文存 [A reservation of Youguang Tu's writings]. 武汉，中国：华中科技大学出版社 [Wuhan: Huazhong University of Science and Technology Press].

Wang, J. (2004). Zhuixun Zhihui zhi Guang 追寻智慧之光 [Seeking wisdom's light]. 高等教育研究 [*Journal of Higher Education*], *25*, 66–67.

Zhang, S. Y. (2002). *Zhexue Daolun* 哲学导论 [*An introduction to philosophy*]. 北京，中国：北京大学出版社 [Beijing: Beijing University Press].

Zhu, X. Z. (2004). Zai Ziwo Shentouzhong Qidi Sixiang 在自我渗透中启迪思想 [Enlightenment Amid Self-permeation]. 高等教育研究 [*Journal of Higher Education*], *25*, 68–69.

Zuo, B., & Lei, H. D. (2015). Tu Youguang Jiaoyu Sixiang Yantaohui Zongshu 涂又光教育思想研讨会综述 [A review of the symposium on the educational thought of Youguang Tu]. 高等教育研究 [*Journal of Higher Education*], *36*, 107–109.

Towards Self-Realisation: Exploring the ecological self for education

CHIA-LING WANG

Abstract

This study examines the concepts of self-realisation and the ecological self in Arne Naess's ecosophy, which considers the manner in which human inherent potentialities are realised in educational practices. This article first elucidates the meaning of the concepts of self-realisation and the ecological self according to Naess's work. Second, the manner of developing the ecological self is discussed by drawing on Buddhist concepts, specifically the advice in the Diamond Sutra. Third, the means of achieving self-realisation is further considered from the view of the Chinese philosophy of Taoism. Both of these Eastern philosophies posit that a clear and peaceful mind can realise the inherent potentialities of the self. With the rapid development of science and technology, education has been unconsciously jeopardised by instrumentalism and consumerism. This has endangered the constitution of modern subjectivity, and engendered an alienated relationship with nature. This article concludes with some thoughts related to this crisis. I conceive of an educational engagement for self-realisation, and argue that a bridge from self-centred to self-realisation is necessary in education.

Introduction

Arne Naess was a Norwegian philosopher who was extensively involved in the study of environmental and ecological matters. His philosophical reflection considered the manner in which humans should lead their lives with nature, in particular through the promotion of his ideal of 'green lifestyles' (Naess, 1989). Naess preferred the term 'ecosophy', rather than 'eco-philosophy', for describing his philosophical concept of ecology. He explained ecosophy in the following manner:

> I mean a philosophy of ecological harmony or equilibrium. A philosophy as kind of sofia [or] wisdom, is openly normative, it contains *both* norms, rules, postulates, value priority announcements *and* hypotheses concerning the state of affairs in our universe. Wisdom is policy wisdom, prescription, not only scientific description and prediction. (Naess, 1995a, p. 8)

Accordingly, Naess's efforts in ecosophy were intended to highlight the dangerous relations between humans and nature and to gain more wisdom to solve environmental crises. In supporting the deep ecology movement, Naess was concerned with the issue of humans' 'life quality' (Naess & Sessions, 1995). Alien from a higher standard of living founded upon economic prosperity, this life quality exists in situations of inherent value. My main interest in this study is exploring the ways of improving life quality through Naess's concepts of self-realisation and the ecological self. In my view, beginning by transforming ourselves as we consider ecological crises is more crucial than appealing to changing the physical environment. This transformation is intended to develop a lifestyle incorporating ecological harmony or ecological wisdom. As in Naess's ecosophy, we must pursue an enhanced life quality by searching for the inherent value in nature. This exploration is also related to a key question by Naess: 'What do you consider to be the ultimate goal or purpose of your life'? (Naess, 1995b, p. 28)

For Naess, self-realisation and the ecological self are connected notions and cannot be discussed separately. Self-realisation is the process of discovering the ecological self, and also a means of practising the ecological self. Naess contributed powerful thoughts to these two concepts. He shifted our viewpoint of nature from anthropocentrism to ecocentrism. This article regards his work as a starting point, and infuses it with elements of Eastern philosophy, specifically to Buddhism and Taoism, to further develop his concepts of self-realisation and the ecological self. The purpose is to attain an in-depth understanding of the significance of the ecological self, and for investigating the approach to achieve self-realisation. As is known, Naess's ecosophy has been heavily influenced by the Buddhist tradition. I also found useful connections between his concepts and Taoism. In the field of education, self-realisation has been used as an educational aim in supporting students to develop their potentialities. Certain Western educationists cling to the notion of psychological analysis, or humanistic psychology's celebrated concept of self-actualisation. This concept stresses psychological growth by manifesting personal latent potentialities. These inquiries of self-realisation, however, ignore the element of ecology or nature that humans inhabit. The realisation of the ecological self has a distinctive significance in education; self-realisation and the ecological self, rather than zealously searching for a way to survive in this world, promote the learning of a better way of being in the world.

In summary, this study explores both the concepts of self-realisation and the ecological self to consider the ultimate goal of life and ponder its implications for educational practice. This article comprises four sections. First, the meaning of the concepts of self-realisation and the ecological self is elucidated, chiefly by drawing upon Naess's work, particularly his inquiry of ecosophy. Second, the manner of self-growth is discussed by drawing upon Buddhist concepts, specifically those in the *Diamond Sutra* (金剛經). These concepts are expected to provide a broader view of the self, which can contribute to a richer account of the ecological self. In addition, the practices of self-realisation involve numerous philosophical questions that warrant investigation. Third, the manner in which self-realisation can be achieved is considered from the viewpoint of Taoism. These explorations are related to the following questions: How can self-realisation be guided? How can individuals open themselves to nature so that identification occurs? What should one attempt to realise in self-realisation? Finally, with the rapid development of science and technology, education has been unconsciously jeopardised by instrumentalism and consumerism. This has endangered the constitution of modern subjectivity, and engendered an alienated relationship with nature. This article concludes by offering some thoughts related to this problem. I argue that self-realisation can be considered an essential objective for educational practices. A bridge from self-centred to self-realisation is necessary in education.

Self-Realisation and the Ecological Self

The concepts of self-realisation and the ecological self were conceived primarily in Naess's article 'Self-realisation: An ecological approach to being in the world' (Naess, 1995b). Naess's inquiry into these notions was motivated by queries about 'who we are, what we are heading for, and what kind of reality we are part of' (Naess, 1995b, p. 13). According to Naess, traditionally, three stages exist for formulating the maturity of the self. Our identities have been in the process of growing from the ego self to the social self, and extending further, from the social self to the metaphysical self. This is a basic process of realising the nature of our being, and the manner in which we relate to each other. However, an obvious problem is that we normally underestimate ourselves because of a narrow ego. We are more self-interestedly concerned with self-requirement than with the needs of others. Most of our conduct aimed at benefitting the self. This causes blindness, in that we cannot see anything other than the self; thus, the connection between the self and others, or the self and nature, is broken. This is what Naess attempted to resolve in his philosophical conception.

Ecological Self

'Everything hangs together' is a crucial concept in Naess's ecosophy (Naess, 1995d). According to Naess, we cannot avoid identifying ourselves with all living beings. Our lives are opened in the process of identification with others. Identification does not merely mean identifying who we are or our status; it entails the notion that we ought to see ourselves in others because, in Naess's ecological view, all species (or even extending to nonspecies) are integrated into wholeness in this world system. Others and I share the same substantial existence. For example, through identification, when I see an injured creature, I feel the sensation of similar trauma in my own body. Another example is that we undergo the identification process with our hometown as we grow up. If we see that this place has been destroyed, through our love for this native place, certain parts of our self are also destroyed. Intense empathy is thus aroused through identification. Because of compassion for others, the boundaries between the self and others dissolve, thus the scope of the self can become broader and deeper. Identification is a humanistic means through which humans can approach natural ecology, and is currently considered to be the attitude that can ultimately resolve environmental crises.

Accordingly, Naess coined the term 'ecological self'. The growth of the ecological self transcends traditional social relationships and is connected with our relationships with nature. In Naess's view, human maturity has to be in, of, and for nature. He described the concept of the ecological self as follows: 'The ecological self of a person is that with which this person identifies'. (Naess, 1995b, p. 15) This means that the self shifts its constitution from the ego, the social self, to that of identification, or rather, the process of identification. Only when the self is immersed into empathetic identification with other beings can it 'persevere in his being' (Naess, 1995b, p. 15). This is a deep life realisation attained by acting out one's own nature, and this deep life realisation goes beyond the lower level requirement of survival.

Self-Realisation

According to Naess, the process of identification is equal to that of self-realisation. Human can realise the nature of the self by means of identification. Self-realisation is a concrete approach of broadening and deepening the ecological self, and elicits care and respect between objects and one's own self. Through self-realisation, the ecological self expands its capability of loving. Naess offers the definition of self-realisation as 'realising inherent potentialities' (Naess, 1995b, p. 18). In this modern free-market society, we are taught to compete with others to triumph in economic competition. The self has become a competitive subject, an excellent pursuer; however, Naess's concept of self-realisation is not realised in this manner. The ways of chasing for social positions and economic advantages can be considered merely as an ego trip, far from the heart of self-realisation. For Naess, individual inherent potentialities are realised through symbiosis rather than competition: 'The maximum success of self-realisation is realised through a certain balance of interactions between organisms and environment' (Naess, 1995c, p. 41). Instead of personal interests, the purpose of self-realisation is for all living beings. Under the global wholeness, only when the ecological system functions well can the individual lead a good life.

The term 'self-realisation' is occasionally capitalised as 'Self-realisation' in Naess's work. This refers to the concept of *atman*—the supreme or universal self derived from Gandhi's philosophy. The ecological self is the *Self* (the Great Self) that approximates the atman concept. The self is what has the capacity to identify. This view is embodied in Naess's assertion of 'biospherical egalitarianism' (Naess, 1995a). Humans were never superior to other beings. Furthermore, we ought to treat each other equally, or even identify with each other in nature. For Naess, this is irrelevant to moral issues or environmental ethics, but he preferred considering biospherical egalitarianism as environmental ontology and realism (Naess, 1995b). The manner in which we treat other beings is akin to the way we treat ourselves. This is not related to comply with moral exhortations. 'All beings are one' (Naess, 2010, p. 199). No differentiation is made between the self and others; only oneness exists under identification. Naess's concept of environmental ontology was inspired by Gestalt thinking, in which 'the whole is greater than the sum of its parts' (Naess, 1995d, p. 241). In Gestalt ontology, the self is regarded not merely as a singular self, but is a self associated with the ecological wholeness.

According to Naess, self-realisation is the ultimate goal in human life and a wise approach for maintaining harmonious relations between the self and nature in the ecosystem. However, one interesting question is as follows: If the goal of self-realisation is to realise inherent potentialities, how can our inherent potentialities be realised? Naess did not clarify this issue in his work. According to Devall's interpretation, 'Ecological self is not a forced or static ideology but rather the search for an opening to nature (Tao) in authentic ways' (Devall, 1995, p. 108). In Devall's view, the intrinsic value of the self could be enlightened by opening ourselves to nature. Next, I discuss this idea of the opening being in nature from the viewpoints of Buddhism and Taoism.

Buddhist Conception of a Clear Mind for Developing the Ecological Self

According to Naess, the concept of the self is not self-centred (Bragg, 1996), but it encourages us to shift away from our personal identity. Drawing on Buddhist thought, Naess considered humans to be constituted by emptiness. Selves 'do not have the concreteness of contents' (Naess, 2010, p. 196); this idea is associated with the Buddhist ontology of the self. Human life is limited and human reception is varied constantly; 'No self can be found, nothing that owns, nothing that belongs' (Conze, 2001). Because of this emptiness, any occurrence is possible. In contrast to the material self, individual spirituality, which composes the eternal self (the original self), can permanently exist. Spirituality enhancement is central to Buddhist self-wakefulness and to Naess's view of self-realisation. Such enhancement can be accomplished by cutting off the consciousness of the self. Only when people are far from self-centred can they engage in their own being and identify themselves with other beings.

Zen Buddhism goes further by demanding that the mind in the Self (*Atman*) should be unoccupied to preserve the original temperament in this physical world. Because of the empty space in the mind, identification with other beings is possible. Greater freedom in the mind of the self expands the greater capacity of identification with others. Once the self has been occupied with substantial content (e.g. persistence, consciousness or interests), it has less capacity to accommodate other beings. This concept has been insightfully elucidated in the Buddhist classic *Diamond Sutra*.

The *Diamond Sutra* is a written record of the dialogue between Buddha and his disciple Subhuti. In this sutra, Subhuti asks Buddha a crucial question: 'When virtuous men or women develop the supreme-enlightenment mind, how should their minds abide and how should they be subdued?' [應云何住？云何降伏其心？] (Lai, 2012) According to Buddha, the highest wisdom of humans is possessing the capability to understand that 'everything with form is unreal' [凡所有象皆是虛妄] (Lai, 2012). This form can be viewed as a variation of the physical phenomena. Any form in this world is 'like a dream, an illusion, a bubble and a shadow, like drops of dew, or flashes of lightning' [如夢幻泡影，如露亦如電] (Lai, 2012); it is vacant in reality, merely a temporary appearance. In our life, it would be wrong to search for, or be persistent as a concrete substance in, this physical world. Buddha said that we 'should develop a mind which does not abide in anything' [應無所住而生其心] (Lai, 2012), thus developing a pure and clear mind that leaves an immeasurable vacancy. A pure mind would not be occupied by substantial forms such as the ego, material ambitions or pursuits based on social value. This does not concern being hollow in the mind but being filled with Buddhist compassion in this vacancy. Rather than being null for practices, this vacancy is filled with humanistic possibilities. This concept inspires the manner of developing the ecological self. The nature of the inner self has no substance; it is only a void for accommodating all beings in the mind. A greater enormity of the self leads to an increased broadness of the mind. The value of the self could be performed by not being conscious of the existence of the self. By transcending the consciousness of 'I', we are able to delve deeper into the intrinsic self. This is the Buddhist teaching regarding how to achieve self-realisation. Taoism has a similar understanding about realising human inherent potentialities without attachment to form, as detailed in the following section.

Taoist Conception of a Peaceful Mind for Self-Realisation

Tao Te Ching (1963), written by the Chinese philosopher Lao-Tzu, is a work of much ecological wisdom. The work's viewpoint is derived from the natural movement of Tao, and it discusses how humans can live a perfect life in harmony with nature. Lao-Tzu encouraged people to seek a peaceful mind and realise the regulation of nature.

> Humans must achieve the ultimate void, and maintain calmness with sincerity to observe the growth and flourishing of all beings. It is in this manner that one can understand the law of nature. [致虛極，守靜篤。萬物並作，吾以觀復。] (See Chapter 16 of *Tao Te Ching*)

For Lao-Tzu, a man can perceive the laws of nature only when he has a peaceful mind. When perceiving the laws of nature, he can act out the original nature of the self. This is similar to Naess's concept of the ecological self. The laws of nature are the so-called *Tao*, according to Lao-Tzu. Tao everlastingly exists with the cosmos. Tao maintains the progress of all beings, including humans, in this ecosystem. The 'void' in Lao-Tzu's account cannot be considered a negative term. It does not mean that we should rid ourselves of any duties or deeds; rather, it reminds people to conduct themselves with less social and psychological desires. A calm life is a life with less desire. Less desire is also a vital value in Naess's concept of deep ecology (Naess, 1995e). When the mind is not hindered by desire, one can eliminate distracting thoughts and spiritually experience all things with clarity. Lao-Tzu expanded on this concept as follows:

> Heaven is everlasting, and earth is enduring. They are everlasting because they do not exist for themselves. Hence, they lead long lives. (天長地久。天地所以能長且久者，以其不自生，故能長生。) (See Chapter 7 of *Tao Te Ching*)

Tao shows us its eminent impartiality by procreating all living beings and caring for all natural beings in an altruistic manner. Following Tao, the temperament of the self should contain the spirit of altruism. When people have less desire in their minds, they are more motivated to prioritise the benefits of all beings, rather than of the private self. Humans are a part of the ecological wholeness. Unselfishness enhances the growth of integrity, and an individual self thus lives longer in this manner. Personal survival is less critical than the proliferation of ecology. Hence, humans should not compete with all other beings, and deprive them of their right to live through excessive human intervention. Taoist philosophy is akin to Gestalt thinking in that it recommends that we look at our life from a holistic viewpoint, which is not limited to anthropocentrism. According to Taoist teaching, a meaningful life is organised for all beings to prosper, without the intention of assuming control. Humans can never survive properly through control or divestments. Only by accepting the regulations of Tao, by following the authentic rule, can life be integrated into nature and thus nature and humans become one. This is the highest harmony with nature that human life can achieve, and is the Taoist way of self-realisation.

Educational Engagement for Self-Realisation

Both Buddhism and Taoism provide insight into coexisting with nature. They delineate what the authentic type of the self could be in associating with nature. According to these philosophies, the nature of the human mind is originally clear and pure, with no complex social or economic interests. However, with the development of the social self, the mind becomes contaminated by a plethora of desires. This contamination prevents human beings' interaction with nature. Only when our mind has been emptied can our capacity for identification be developed and the ecological self realise its potentialities. In the philosophy of Tao, humans are a part of nature. Humans do not exist merely out of self-interest but to manifest the implications of Tao. This is the ideal 'green lifestyle', as termed by Naess. However, how can we think of this lifestyle in educational practice? What is the significance of the ecological self or self-realisation in education?

The concept of education has been influenced substantially by scientific development. Modern technology has transformed education into its current form, which pursues effectiveness and economic utility. In educational practice, most considerations involve inspiring human motivation for self-growth. However, this self-growth has been narrowly interpreted as achieving individual social desires such as material fortunes, status and reputation. Education has been an effective approach for satisfying these requirements. Instead of harmonious relationships, students learn more about competition with others, and they treat nature in the same fashion. Consequently, the current educational systems directly or indirectly produce a distorted attitude towards human life. This crisis has been exacerbated by the increased roles of the ideologies of instrumentalism and consumerism in education.

In *The Three Ecologies* (Guattari, 2012), Félix Guattari provided similar critique of an insidious trend that he called Integrated World Capitalism (IWC). He described IWC as a new industrial power exercised over the media and advertising. IWC arose out of free-market competition and normalised our lives. Human beings thus turn into the 'dominant capitalistic subjectivity' (Pindar & Sutton, 2012). The educational system is one of the new productive assemblages through which the ecology of subjectivity is mentally manipulated by the capitalist ideology for the pursuit of material interests. Guattari's conception views the three ecologies, namely the environment, social relations and human subjectivity, as three related elements that are inseparable.

Human subjectivity has close connection with its exteriority, including social ecology in schools and the living environment in nature. Following Guattari's view, educational system should not play the role of trapping human subjectivity within an inactive ecology or cycle of deathly repetition.

How can education aid in cultivating an active ecology without ideological or mental hindrance, and facilitate individual self-realisation? Following Naess's ecosophy, bridge from self-love to self-realisation can be constructed through education. Self-love is the foundation of individual growth; however, it invariably confined the self to the narrow ego, or becomes self-centred. By contrast, self-realisation can serve as a higher purpose in education. It is reached by deselfing or eliminating self-consciousness to create a broadness of the self. Rather than inspiring students' motivation to seek what they desire, education could promote the emptying of the mind through a reduction in desire. According to Buddhism and Taoism, only an empty mind can create unlimited possibilities for human life. A clear and pure mind is essential for engaging in identification and self-realisation. How should the individual mind dwell? Instead of personal requirements, an ecological self should dwell on the rule of nature, and on all beings, as Devall noted:

> Nature needs us as life-affirming people. Affirmation of our own self-realizing ecological self embraces more and more of the 'other' into ourself. The more open, receptive, vulnerable, adventurous we are, the more we affirm the integrity of being-in-the-world. (Devall, 1995, p. 116)

These life-affirming people could be the primary emphasis in ecological education, or even in life education. Regarding teaching practices, educators could organise more activities for students to learn harmonious cooperation with other fellow students. Furthermore, experience to be with and in nature facilitates learning how to embrace other beings in this world.

Conclusion

This article explores Naess's concept of self-realisation and the ecological self, and considers the manner in which humans' inherent potentialities can be realised in educational practice. Buddhism and Taoism are employed to interpret these two concepts and elucidate a clearer approach for actualising these concepts in human life. The Buddhist classic the *Diamond Sutra* provides a means of purifying our mind for developing the ecological self. Lao-Tzu's *Tao Te Ching* inspires a peaceful mind for accomplishing the ideal of self-realisation. Both texts present a deep and rich means of becoming harmonious with nature.

According to Naess, we need a 'deep ecological attitude' (Naess, 1995f). This attitude is also a green lifestyle. It supports us in countering the dangers of materialism and consumerism. In the face of current ecological crises, the primary task is perhaps not eradicating all behaviour that is harmful to our environment. According to Naess's ecosophy, as well as the Buddhist and Taoist concepts of the self, what should be fundamentally adjusted is human attitude towards nature. Environmental change can be triggered by the inner self. The purpose of educational practice can be shifted from one that is self-centred to self-realisation. What we seek is a broader concept of the ecological self, not merely a socially self-actualised self.

Disclosure statement

No potential conflict of interest was reported by the author.

Funding

This research was sponsored by the Ministry of Science and Technology, Taiwan [grant number 103-2410-H-019-013-].

References

Bragg, E. A. (1996). Towards ecological self: Deep ecology meets constructionist self-theory. *Journal of Environmental Psychology, 16*, 93–108.
Conze, E. (2001). *Buddhist wisdom: The diamond sutra and the heart sutra*. New York, NY: Vintage Books.
Devall, B. (1995). The ecological self. In A. Drengson & Y. Inoue (Eds.), *The deep ecology movement: An introductory anthology* (pp. 101–123). Berkeley, CA: North Atlantic Books.
Guattari, F. (2012). *The three ecologies* (I. Pindar & P. Sutton, Trans.). London: Continuum. (Original work published 1989)
Lai, Y. H. (2012). *The Heart Sutra, Diamond Sutra* (Q. P. Chen, Trans.). Taipei City: Linking books.
Lao-Tzu. (1963). *Tao Te Ching: The greatest wisdom of Lao-Tzu* (T. Sun, Trans.). San Francisco, CA: Chi Chu Moral Culture and Education Foundation.
Naess, A. (1989). The environmental crisis and the deep ecological movement. In A. Naess (Ed.), *Ecology, community and lifestyle* (pp. 23–34). Cambridge: Cambridge University Press.
Naess, A. (1995a). The shallow and deep, long-range ecology movement: A summary. In A. Drengson & Y. Inoue (Eds.), *The deep ecology movement: An introductory anthology* (pp. 3–9). Berkeley, CA: North Atlantic Books.
Naess, A. (1995b). Self-realisation: An ecological approach to being in the world. In A. Drengson & Y. Inoue (Eds.), *The deep ecology movement: An introductory anthology* (pp. 13–30). Berkeley, CA: North Atlantic Books.
Naess, A. (1995c). The systematization of the logically ultimate norms and hypotheses of Ecosophy T. In A. Drengson & Y. Inoue (Eds.), *The deep ecology movement: An introductory anthology* (pp. 31–48). Berkeley, CA: North Atlantic Books.
Naess, A. (1995d). Ecosophy and gestalt ontology. In G. Sessions (Ed.), *Deep ecology for the twenty-first century* (pp. 240–245). Boston, MA: Shambhala.
Naess, A. (1995e). Deep ecology and lifestyle. In G. Sessions (Ed.), *Deep ecology for the twenty-first century* (pp. 259–261). Boston, MA: Shambhala.

Naess, A. (1995f). Deep ecology for the twenty-second century. In G. Sessions (Ed.), *Deep ecology for the twenty-first century* (pp. 463–467). Boston, MA: Shambhala.

Naess, A. (2010). Gestalt thinking and Buddhism. In A. Drengson & B. Devall (Eds.), *The ecology of wisdom: Writings by Arne Naess* (pp. 195–203). Berkeley, CA: Counterpoint.

Naess, A., & Sessions, G. (1995). Platform principles of the deep ecology movement. In A. Drengson & Y. Inoue (Eds.), *The deep ecology movement: An introductory anthology* (pp. 49–53). Berkeley, CA: North Atlantic Books.

Pindar, I., & Sutton, P. (2012). Translators' introduction. In F. Guattari (Ed.), *The three ecologies* (pp. 1–11). London: Continuum.

Contextualising Postmodernity in Daoist Symbolism: Toward a mindful education embracing eastern wisdom

Rob Blom & Chunlei Lu ⓘ

Abstract

In cultivating a Western inclination toward Eastern wisdom, it is important to seek the foundations that sustain traditional practices toward such end. In a secularised and modern world view, the tendency has been to extract and abstract foundational practices such as mindfulness meditation and contemplation within an objectivist or scientist prejudice. While leading to interesting results, it cannot ascertain a wisdom that is quantified and decontextualised. In response, contextual effort in postmodern pedagogical literature—while well placed—is often marred with confusions concerning Eastern and metaphysical foundations. As a result, one is led away from the very wisdom being qualified; furthermore, conceptual and theoretical paradoxes arise and consequently elude those that formulate them. Thus, in feeling secure in response to a particular 'yáng' world view of modernity, many postmodern criticisms suffer an exclusively 'yīn' character. For us, imbalance in any direction forfeits the path Eastern education approaches wisdom. In our conceptual analysis, we contextualise that modernity was never too yáng, but too yáng-in-yīn. Therefore, what is missing in pedagogical theory is not the yīn element, as presumed by postmodern critique, but the yáng element, in continual balance with the yīn, and vice versa.

In resonance with an interconnected, holistic—and dare we say postmodern—worldview, one may ascertain that 'the farthest West is but the farthest East' (Smith, 2006); but taking a page from Rudyard Kipling, we could also say 'East is East, and West is West, and never the twain shall meet.' While any systematic or philosophical thought will have its antithesis—especially one of extremes—it may be prudent to justify the middle path, with, perhaps, a slight leaning toward one or the other depending upon one's situated hermeneutic context. For the purpose of our criticism, we wish to attenuate the former perspective which too hastily connects East and West.

In cultivating a Western inclination toward Eastern wisdom, it is important to seek the foundations that sustain traditional practices toward such end. In a secularised and modern(ised) world view, the tendency has been to extract and abstract foundational practices like mindfulness meditation and contemplation within an objectivist or scientistic prejudice (Blom, Lu, & Mgombelo, 2015). While leading to interesting results, it cannot ascertain a wisdom that is *quantified* and *decontextualised*. In response, *contextual* effort in postmodern pedagogical literature—while well placed—is often marred with confusions concerning Eastern and metaphysical foundations. As a result, one is led away from the very wisdom being *qualified*. Furthermore, conceptual and theoretical paradoxes arise and consequently elude those that formulate them. Thus, in feeling secure in response to a particular '*yáng*' (阳) world view of modernity—advocating against what is masculine, certain, mechanical, hierarchical, patriarchal, and so on— many postmodern criticisms suffer an exclusively *yīn* (阴) character. For us, imbalance in any direction forfeits the path Eastern education approaches wisdom (*sophia, zhìhuì*, 智慧).

Utilising Daoist symbolism, we aim to encapsulate postmodernist trends, their supposed critiques against modernity, and the subtle contextualisation we 'unEarthed' from their combination (see Figure 2). From our exploration, an immediate consequence arises: modernity was never too *yáng*, but too '*yáng*-in-*yīn*;' and with our concluding conceptual map, we encourage future pedagogy theorists interested in Eastern wisdom—in a Westernised light—to recognise an integral *yīn-yáng* balance. It is within the context of metaphysics to which Eastern mindfulness (*sati, niàn*, 念) and wisdom—a balance of character and discerning intelligence[1] (*zhì*, 智)—rightfully belong.

Postmodern Criticism of Modernity as 'Too *Yáng*' is Really 'Too *Yáng*-in-*Yīn*'

As a historical epoch after modernity, postmodernity denotes the state of a society or individual as being postmodern. However, postmodernity has been argued as a continuation *of*—and thus within—modernity, or as a cultural backlash *against* modernity and the state of being modern; thus, any strict definition of a postmodern theorist is elusive. Nonetheless, a common critique held against modernity has been its anachronistic qualities present in our world. Modes of thinking that are rational, analytic, reductionist, and linear, and value systems that are competitive, quantitative, and domineering are labelled as 'masculine' (*yáng*); its feminine (*yīn*) counterpart contrasts thinking as intuitive, synthetic, holistic, and nonlinear, encompassed in a value system of cooperation and (e)quality (Capra, 1997, p. 10). These intersubjective qualities seem equally enmeshed in an interobjective science of the biosphere—colloquially termed the 'web of life'—and the tenets of deep ecology, typified by irreducible wholes, networks, interrelationships, and interdependencies.

Prevalent across deep ecological (ecomasculinist) and ecofeminist attitudes is a re-enchantment with the feminine (*yīn*) principle; we could also say a re-enchantment with Nature,[2] Earth, or our bodies (in contrast to mind). The 'disenchantment' may well have been under way since agrarian times, however, Eco-Romantic critique is often levelled toward decontextualised 'absolutes' or 'universals' inherited from the Ego-Enlightenment thinkers of seventeenth-century modernity. As Toulmin (1990) ascertained, 'one aim of seventeenth-century philosophers [Descartes and contemporaries] was to frame all their questions in terms that rendered them *independent of context*[3] [emphasis added]' (p. 21); the consequence of four centuries of reductionist scientific thinking, *sub specie æternitatis*,[4] is that *certainty* replaced *humanism*, *formal logic* replaced *rhetoric*, and *permanence*[5] replaced the *transitory*. For better and worse, these absolutes are in part due to the reflection paradigm with the emergence of reason as the centre of social gravity (Wilber, 2000). In the latter case, reason succumbed to rationality and confined itself to empiric-analytic, objectifying, monological,[6] or positivistic modes—hence 'absolutes' were studied separate from the Cartesian notion of the 'thinking thing' (*res cogitans*): a mind *dissociated* from body. Over time, a reductionist (intersubjective) culture birthed its social (interobjective) counterpart: the mechanical and uniform(ing) era of industry. The industrial age saw the world metaphorically as a *machine* devoid of life and 'based on the assumption of separability and manipulability' (Shiva, 1989, p. 22). Metaphysically, 'industry is really the opposite of "true craft" as the partisans of "progress" so readily declare, a "thing of the past". The workman in industry cannot put into his work anything of himself' (Guénon, 1946/2004, p. 60). Therefore:

> The machine is in a sense the opposite of the tool, and is in no way a 'perfected tool' as many imagine, for the tool is in a sense a 'prolongation' of the man himself, whereas the machine reduces the man to being no more than its servant; and, if it was true to say that 'the tool engenders the craft' it is no less true that the machine kills it.[7] (p. 60)

Historically, the appeal for mass-production—a truly quantitative notion—did not limit itself to industry, but extended to branches of both science in the form of *predictive power* and Westernised education in the form of *schooling* and *discipline* (Davis, 2004).[8] In classroom 'mechanics,' (so-called *yáng*) metaphors of maximisation, efficiency, output, uniformity, certitude, and control stood deliberate as quantifiers of positivist (input-output) *learning*; the 'neglect is manifest, for example, in scientific technologies that are deployed in ignorance of their environmental consequences … and in educational systems structured around age-appropriate (vs. situation- or person-appropriate) standardised curricula' (p. 161). Even in pedagogical research, uniformity persists to statistically maintain quantifiers.

Within the information age is the recognition that the whole system is *more* than the sum of its abstracted parts; contrasted to reductionism comes 'systems thinking' or 'environmental (contextual) thinking' (Capra, 1997). Co-incidentally, Nature (*physis*, φύσις) as *manifestation* etymologically implies *becoming* and evolution, which we see ubiquitously in paradigmatic science today. For physics, a Cartesian–Newtonian legacy of *time-independent* equations is replaced with *time-irreversible* probability densities $\rho(r, t)$ in credit to Ilya Prigogine, whose dissipative structures and bifurcation theory, moreover, affected the domain of chemistry. In cellular biology we see *autopoiesis* (ατο-, 'self' + ποίησις, 'creation, production') and at the fundamental level of math appears Tarski and Gödel's incompleteness theorems, chaos theory, complexity (nonlinear dynamics), and fractals. Each have elements of *in*determinacy, *un*predictability, *in*completeness, or *un*certainty. As Capra (1997) noted, the use of negating prefixes show how deeply ingrained Cartesian–Newtonian concepts are in our scientific mentality! Perhaps Heraclitus said it best: *no person ever steps into the same river twice.*

One may ponder the *raison d'être* for a mechanical, parts-based approach to knowledge, which undeniably underlies the compartmentalisation of education, agriculture, science, and so on. Perhaps we had to stray to recognise the inherent errors of our scientific assumptions and *beliefs*—making science—and the education that supports it —an evolving knowledge system.[9] Could reductionist, quantitative, and uniforming tendencies have matched a consciousness that reflected the mental habits of centuries past? Habits presumably '*yáng*' and 'modern' from the vantage of postmodern lenses? Today, *holistic* or *wholistic* (*ecological*) metaphors of optimisation, embodiment, diversity, and creativity abound. Educationally, a 'learning system' becomes an 'enactive system;' biologically, 'personal learning is not about acquisition, processing, or storing, but about emergent structuring' (p. 165). Similarly, embodiment practices that emphasise mindful participation focuses on the reconnection between mind and body (Lodewyk, Lu, & Kentel, 2009). In summary, ecological postmodern literature advocates difference, multiplicity, diversity, and communion over *agency* and *uniformity*. These are among many trends we perceive to be beneficial arising from the reclamation of the feminine (*yīn*) principle. However, can reclamation infer a *yīn* tendency replaces a *yáng*? In Daoist theory, *yīn* and *yáng* are relative, harmoniously coexisting toward development as contraries (restrictive) or from a higher perspective as complementaries (facilitative); their roles *in manifestation* are not fixed, and although in continual integration *yīn* and *yáng* may exchange their positions, we find this unlikely and look toward the reclamation of the *yáng*; in absence of metaphysics, we place the inevitably paradoxes from the *yīn* imbalance under scrutiny.

Conceptual Errors and Paradoxes of the *yīn* Imbalance

According to Wilber (2000), *the* central problem of modernity has been how human subjectivity (as will and agency) relates to the world; put differently, how do mind and body relate? The Ego-Enlightenment camp stressed autonomy against *heteronomy* so moral freedom could prevail over amoral nature; reason, they argued, birthed *individualism* and allowed the mind to transcend biospheric inclinations—a *differentiation* of the mind from body. It was reason (through the rational-ego) that rose to worldcentric compassion above egocentric and ethnocentric drives relating to an amoral nature (and Nature). Thus, an autonomous ego or self-defining subject coupled a cultural emergence of *moral* consciousness; moral life became equivalent to *freedom* from a mind differentiated from body (Wilber, 2000). Conversely, Eco-Romantics argued against *propositional truth* arising from autonomous reflection on Nature, emphasised *truthfulness* through embodied expression, and *participatory* communion over agentic isolation. Unity and wholeness were to be found in sympathy and Nature—a point the Ego camp would chastise as *regressive*; likewise, against the Ego camp, a subjectivity denoted in (a false) absolute language denigrates the emancipatory potential of rationality to forms of control, domination, *repression* (of body), and so on (Wilber, 2000).

Rationality, as it originated, meant 'the capacity for [universal] perspectivism, for sustained introspection, and for imagining "as-if" and "what-if" possibilities.

Rationality [was] the sustained capacity for cognitive pluralism and perspectivism' (Wilber, 2001, p. 229). However, the universal perspectivism (*yīn-yáng* balance) that initiated the Ego-Enlightenment era collapsed to universal (too *yáng*-in-*yīn*): an atomistic *uniformity (absolutism-in-naturalism)* where homogenisation diluted world-centric perspectives to one for all cultures (what is good for me is good for everyone). Conversely, the celebration of diversity (perspectives) from the Eco-Romantics 'started from the same rational stance of *universal perspectivism*, but it emphasised the "perspectives" instead of the "universal"' (p. 483), becoming too *yīn* (Figure 3). Each position became irreducible contraries—a subsequent dualism (the more of one, the less of the other)—that led to respective paradoxes and pathologies.

For the Eco camp, extreme diversity slid into divine egoism (all are unique), begetting agentic isolation; regarding *hypercommunion*, one loses sense of self and diverse community succumbs to uniforming world-views. For the Ego camp, 'the holism of nature produced the atomism of the self' (Wilber, 2000, p. 441), leaving the subject 'I' disengaged in non-participatory communion by its own self-defining agency; an agency, moreover, whose function depended upon the very communion it *repressed*.[10] Moreover, to preserve its own *transcended* autonomy, the rational-ego not only repressed the body, but discarded further transcendence toward the psychic (ψυχή, *psuche*) and subtle(r) stages of self-sense development (and thus greater autonomy); therefore, the freedom it sought became *unfreedom* by denying anything hierarchical beyond egoic-rationality (*trans*-rationalities). Educationally, we see *hyperagency* in the goal of critical pedagogues who espouse universal emancipation, specifically against an anti-environmental industrial paradigm. Seeing previous generations and ideologies as oppressive, universal emancipation then implicates the anti-environmental position by assuming the 'loss of intergenerational knowledge and networks of mutual aid [are] a necessary part of becoming modern' (Bowers, 2010, p. 5). Therefore, 'by ignoring that the life supporting characteristics of natural systems are in decline, they can maintain the myth that each generation will become more enlightened and self-directing' (p. 11).

To remedy these deficiencies and paradoxes requires depth (*hierarchy*) and the concept of a *holon* (ὄλον; from the Greek neuter form *holos*, 'ὅλος, whole'). A holon is neither a whole nor a part, but simultaneously a whole/part comprising four quadrants (Figure 1) and coupled with its own relative agency and communion; through greater depth, a holon transcends to meet its relative agentic and communal deficiencies, *ad indefinītum*. For example, a holon at the world-centric stage for moral development will perceive and act in the world that encompasses (and transcends) an ethnocentric stage; this is true for any developmental line: cognitive, affective, self-identity, or so on. If a holon becomes too whole (hyperagency) or too much a part (hypercommunion), pathology ensues. Balance is preferably to vacillation, and stillness gives rise to transcendence.

Concerning 'transformative' education, *a theoretical impasse* between self-responsible agency (critical pedagogy theorists) and self-abnegating communion (ecological pedagogy theorists) subsists—precisely because neither are transformational. Instead, agency and communion are *horizontal* and restrictive, thereby *translational* movements;[11] ecological sensitivity 'is about *lateral* or *outward* relationships as opposed to

A KALEIDOSCOPIC VIEW OF CHINESE PHILOSOPHY OF EDUCATION

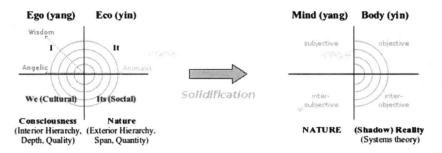

Figure 1: Adaptation of Integral Model showcasing solidification toward the exclusively *yīn* and quantitative

Notes: In a monological or flatland worldview, no interpretation and no mutual understanding exists, only 'surfaces' without any *value*. Hierarchy or depth (*within*), represented by concentric circles, becomes replaced by heterarchy and a flatland ontology (Wilber, 2000). On the right, a disengaged subject reflects on a pre-given world; a rational-ego may say it is part of interlocking web, but doing so collapses interior depth (subjective sphere) to the empirical dimension. Similarly systems theory (interobjective), albeit nonreductionist, suffers from *subtle reductionism:* a span-oriented collapse of interiority (*yáng*) to exteriority (*yīn*). In absence of Selfhood, the Light of Plato's Cave is confused for the sum of the shadows (Wilber, 2000). Therefore, we are without a Westernised context for wisdom and growth in consciousness (NATURE) in objectivist and scientist lenses.

forward or *upward* grasping [emphases added]' (Davis, 2004, p. 160). While eighty to ninety percent of experiential growth *is* translational, what masks (and hinders) *vertical* transformation ('passage beyond form') is that

> self-adaptation and self-transcendence [are referred to] *interchangeably* [emphasis added], because both embody a type of 'going beyond'. But apart from that similarity, the two are different in degree and in kind. In self-adaptation or communion, one finds oneself to be *part* of a *larger* whole; in self-transformation one *becomes a new whole*, which has its own new forms of agency (relative autonomy) *and* communion. (Wilber, 2000, p. 50)

According to Wilber (2000), most web-of-life theorists wish to 'equate a *finite* and *temporal nature* with an *infinite* and *eternal Spirit* [emphases added]' (p. 294). The idea of *translative* learning systems as open, adaptive, and enactive, is insufficient without the transformative (*angelic*) dimension within: 'it would be absurd to say that man, as man and by human means, can surpass himself' (Guénon, 1927/2004, p. 206). Therefore, we can classify the metaphysical context for *sati* of the East as oriented toward the subtle or *yáng* and the mindfulness of the West as oriented toward the gross or *yīn* (Figure 2).

On Metaphysics and the Possibility of Integration

Historically, the modern calamity was reducing 'all introspective and interpretive knowledge to exterior and empirical flatland: [erasing] the richness of interpretation from the script of the world' (Wilber, 2000, p. 162); epistemic truth became independent from who presents it and to whom; 'for Descartes and his successors, timely questions were no concern of philosophy: instead, their aim was to bring to light *per-*

manent structures underlying all the *changeable* phenomena of Nature [emphasis added]' (Toulmin, 1990, p. 34). The drive to bring immutable structures (read: absolutes) into mutable conditions (read: naturalism) suffers from a misplaced metaphysical heritage of late Scholasticism. In short, we consider absolutism-in-naturalism—leading to uniformity, permanence, and so on—as too *yáng*-in-*yīn* (pseudo-metaphysics), rather than too *yáng* in the context of metaphysics (Figure 3).

Postmodernists, on the other hand, 'would go to extraordinary lengths to deny depth [hierarchy] in general' (Wilber, 2000, p. 169). Without hierarchy—and greater discernment—all perspectives became equally valid. From a metaphysical perspective, anti-spiritual tendencies led to the *solidification* of the being and to conceptions of uniformity, atomism, and individualism (Guénon, 1945/2004); what followed was subsequent *self-dissolution*, rather than *self-transcendence:* a solid, atomistic shell led to a hollow one. Worse, since span was the only metric (bigger is better), ecological and complexity educational discourses (must) situate mind *in* the body (Figure 2);[12] thus we are *part* of what Davis (2004) calls a 'more-than-human' (*whole*) Earth. The contradiction that aims to regain a (qualitative) humanistic world while simultaneously placing humans within a horizontal, biocentric web-of-life is a severe conceptual error based upon a depthless view of the cosmos. As a result, with mindbody differentiation as the 'great mistake' (read: disenchantment), union with pre-conventional Nature via empirical-sensory awareness (*environmental instinct*,[13] 直觉) caricatured a mind body *integration* (union) of post-conventional Spirit (*intellectual intuition*, 智的直覺). Eco-Romantically, the perspective of Earth as 'more-than-human' is alluring simply because the spatial metric is (perceived to be) more encompassing. But Eco-Noetically (traditionally), the Earth is *less*-than-human based upon the higher perspective of

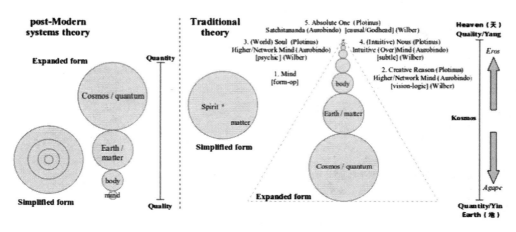

Figure 2: The cosmos vs. the (Pythagorean) Kosmos

Notes: Each circle represents a successive (*holonic*) stage of consciousness or *fulcrum* (self-sense) for development. Conceptually, no capability of Eros or Ascent (transformation) exists in a Westernised (left) perception as Earth 'transcends' us as a 'more-than-human' and emergent phenomena. However, as we expand perception from {span} to {span, depth}, we correlate with traditional symbolism by placing humans between Heaven and Earth. The centre dot representing Spirit is subject to inverted spatial symbolism as it lies beyond space and time. Of note is the simplified form of systems theory which exemplifies our ecological too *yáng*-in-*yīn* critique (mind-in-body; more-than-human Earth; and so on) symbolised in Figure 3.

span *and* depth (Figure 2). Since unity was theorised in the Each and the All (systems approach) and not the One, a false spirituality (metaphysics) was developed, one ecological as opposed to intellectual.

As Wilber (2000) apprises, a qualitative distinction exists between differentiation and eventual *integration* (good), and *dissociation* (bad). In the Westernised context, linking mind with body through mindfulness may reverse dissociation (*yīn* tendency), but integration is accomplished in view of the trans-rational (*yáng* tendency). While modern science simply extracts and abstracts meditative practices such as mindfulness, in the Eastern context, mindfulness 'is the beginning of virtually all paths of contemplation, the aim of which is the remembering that one's true nature is Buddha-nature' (p. 339). Thus, *sati* resembles the Platonic *reminiscence:* 'that which is simply "learned" from the outside is quite valueless in the former case, however great may be the quantity of the notions accumulated; ... what counts is, on the contrary, an "awakening" of the latent possibilities that the being carries in itself' (Guénon, 1945/2004, p. 59). Thus, what accompanied traditional—as opposed to modern—*theōría (contemplatio)* was a corresponding 'realisation.'

Metaphysical discernment is limited in the West,[14] primarily displaced by philosophical and religious treatises. The confusion between the study of ephemeral nature (*physis*) and the study beyond (sensory) nature (*metaphysis* from μετά, 'beyond') is based upon a particular ignorance[15] (*avidyā*)—one allegorised by Plato's Cave—rather than an inaccuracy of the modern and postmodern 'spirit' (or lack thereof). In the traditional, pre-modern West, a 'nature' that lay beyond playfulness (*līlā*) took on a sacred (*sacratum*) character, which is connected by no mere coincidence to secret (*secretum*) and mystery (*musterion*) which both designate silence and the *inexpressible*. As Guénon (1946/2004) expounded, *sacratum* and *secretum* both derive from the Latin *secernere* ('to place apart, put aside') which discerns (*discere*, 'to learn') the sacred from the profane. A deeper interpretation of *musterion* 'designates what must be received in silence' (p. 122) as seen in monastic and mystical orders. Spatially, 'a consecrated place is called *templum*, of which the root *tem* (found in the Greek *temno*, 'to cut,' 'to cut off from,' 'to separate,' from which *temenos*, 'a sacred enclosure,' is derived)' (p. 122). Contemplation, deriving from the root *tem*, strictly denotes an inwardness (*depth*), on the order beyond space and time, that is, toward the timeless and eternal.

Now the 'timeless "Nature" (Plato's διαιώνια φύσις) [is] distinguished from its temporal manifestations, which is the distinction of the stasis of that which is from the motion-and-rest of things that become' (Coomaraswamy, 1987, p. 65). Stasis (non-acting) cannot be rest (non-moving) as the latter depends upon spatiality. Manifestation at rest is truly *frozen* in an unstable equilibrium (too *yáng*-in-*yīn*). The general pattern we see is that those grown up upon a false eternal framework of *uniformity* and universals, blame Plato (or modernity), and abandon metaphysics *despite having never followed his educational thesis!* Consider what Plato himself wrote in the Seventh Epistle:

> I can affirm about any present or future writers who pretend to knowledge of the matters with which I concern myself [mystical knowledge of the One]; in my judgment *it is impossible that they should have any understanding*

of the subject. It is not something that can be put into words like other branches of learning; only after long partnership in a common life [contemplative community] devoted to this very thing does truth flash upon the soul, like a flame kindled by a leaping spark. *No treatise by me concerning it exists or ever will exist* [emphasis added]. (as cited in Wilber, 2000, p. 329)

In other words, the Dao that one speaks of is not the true Dao as 'those who know don't talk; those who talk don't know' (*Dào Dé Jīng*, 56, Red Pine translation). Truth is *incommunicable* and mystery *inexpressible* in the truest and most profound sense of the word. Certainty of objective truth is relative to certainty found in the union of our innermost Being (Schuon, 1970/2009). While the information age attempts to disentangle secrets and make everything 'known'—it must humbly accept one secret—*and it just so happens to be the very goal of Plato's educational journey toward wisdom.*

A key characteristic in traditional science (metaphysics) is the emphasis placed upon *qualitative* hierarchy (*scala naturæ*), *consciousness*, and *depth* toward which mindfulness practices are directed. While natural science acknowledges *quantitative* hierarchy (mineral, plant, animal), metaphysicians placed relative import to the lower, quantitative domain due to its correspondence to the higher.[16] To Guénon (1945/2004), modern science 'only takes account of the lower [domains], and being incapable of passing beyond the domain to which it is related, claims to reduce all reality to it' (p. 5). Such subtle reductionism toward an 'exclusively quantitative character [has] now become assimilated to that of purely mathematical theories [which] takes them yet further away from the sensible reality that they claim to explain, [one] situated on a lower plane than that of sensible reality' (p. 166). Now, the solution to uniformity or sameness on the surface (too *yáng*-in-*yīn*) and diversity and the loss of sameness within (too *yīn*) is the *holonic* unit since uniformity (as pure quantity) is only a caricature of unity (as pure quality) whose true(r) reflection resides in the *unit* (Guénon, 1946/2004). As a *disqualified unit* spread homogeneously thin, uniformity takes on *instrumental value* as seen in agriculture, education, and so on. Similarly, the *immobility* (of rocks) is a caricature of the *immutability* of Spirit; while timely questions concern the temporal order, timelessness concerns the non-manifest order.

We can relate the traditional relationship between quality and quantity to Daoist symbolism, where manifestation occurs between two poles hierarchically arranged as Earth (*Di*, 地) supporting manifestation below[17] and Heaven (*Tiān*, 天) covering manifestation above[18] (see Figure 2). Heaven (pure *Yáng*) and Earth (pure *Yīn*) are the primordial duality[19] of manifestation, representing the *active* (masculine) and *passive* (feminine) principles respectively.[20] Prior to their macro-cosmic differentiation is *Tàijí* ('pinnacle,' 太极) known in Western Scholasticism as Being, Essence, or the realm of possibilities of manifestation. Being lies beyond manifestation, unaffected by its manifest qualities and thus exemplifies a property of immutability. The realm of possibilities of non-manifestation is comprised in Non-Being or *Wújí* ('without pinnacle,' 无极), the principle of Being. Finally, the principle connecting these within Universal Possibility is the *Dào* (道). For this reason, non-Duality is greater than Unity. When we add *Rén* ('human,' 人) and place it between *Di* and *Tiān*, we get the ternary *Tiān-Di-Rén* (天地人) depicting *Rén* as the Son or Daughter of Heaven and Earth. While

Tàijí combines Heaven and Earth *qua principle*, *Rén* as a reflection of *Tàijí* combines Heaven and Earth *qua resultant*. But if we consider the ternary *Tiān-Rén-Di* (天人地) the role of *Rén* now becomes the *mediator* or *bridge* between these poles (Guénon, 1946/1991) with manifold applications in Daoist training.[21] Ergo, we are not part of Earth, but Earth is part of us (Figure 2), and we are part of the higher *hypostasis* of Spirit. However, without depth, and under quantitative and empirical zeal, we become much more *terrestrial* Sons and Daughters of Earth (too *yīn*). However, it is these *celestial* spheres (*yáng* tendency) where 'non-human' wisdom originates and mindbody integration occurs. Similarly, on the basis of intellectual intuition (supra-rationality), metaphysicians would offer their own critique against rationality while simultaneously contextualising the Eco camp as *sub*rational (*e*-motive).

Contextualising Reason and the Possibility of Transcendence

Our present understanding of metaphysics has either been marred by—and mistaken for—Cartesian *mechanism* (pseudo-metaphysics) or confused with *metaphysical realism* (modern science), neither which are universal, but rather representational, natural, and positive. Confusing the Cartesian–Newtonian (mechanical) notion, Davis (2004) exemplifies the postmodern perspective: 'the study of metaphysics, for Aristotle, had to do with the identification of unchanging laws and principles that govern forms and phenomena *that exist in the realm of the physical* [emphasis added]' (p. 16). Davis elaborated that 'since Aristotle's time, metaphysics has been taken up and applied in ways that depart from the original meaning' (p. 16). We can hardly miss pointing out his role in doing so![22] And while Aristotle placed greater emphasis on reason, it was as the human reflection of the Logos—as evident from the etymology of *logic*—and not modern logic generally attributed to Aristotle today as a form of rationalism 'evolved' or 'refined' therefrom (Schuon, 1970/2009). In believing that the culmination of Aristotelian logic leads to modern logic as, at last, 'mature and efficacious … they [the evolutionary rationalists] obviously are unaware that this flowering of a discipline of thought, while having its merits, *goes more or less hand in hand with a weakening, or even an atrophy, of intellectual intuition* [emphasis added]' (p. 7)! Rectifying matters, Guénon (1924/2004) would unequivocally state:

> Descartes limited intelligence to reason, that he granted to what he thought might be called 'metaphysics' the mere function of serving as a basis for physics, and that this physics itself was by its very nature destined, in his eyes, to pave the way for the applied sciences, mechanical, medicinal, and moral—the final limit of human knowledge as he conceived it. (pp. 11, 12)

The other error in Cartesian mechanism was the mind-body dualism it implied; yet such dualism is levelled against Plato—despite being a nondualist—through an unfortunate (mis)interpretation of his *Meno*.[23] For instance, we read: 'Plato's assertion that this world is an imperfect shadow of a nonsensorial ideal realm would seem to be implicated in the conceptual separation of mind and body' (Davis, 2004, p. 149). Ironically, Plato considered reason *opinion*, and distinction was made between *pure Intellect* (*buddhi*)—*aliquid increatum et increabile*—and its impure instrument (*manas*);

buddhi (*nous*, νους)—the order of intellectual intuition—arises when *manas* 'is brought to rest in its own source (*cittaṃ svayonāv upaśāmyate*) by a surcease from fluctuation' (Coomaraswamy, 1987, p. 211) so that *gnosis* is reached through dementation (*amanībhāva*) when 'there is no longer a distinction of Knower from Known or of Knowledge and Being, but only a Knowledge as Being and a Being as Knowledge' (p. 212). Therefore, a necessity for Plato was to move beyond the discursiveness of reason—as *mediate* knowledge—to what is grasped immediately *in divinis*.

Now the postulates of rationalism are essentially defined, by all its forms, whether philosophical rationalism or otherwise, as 'a *belief* in the supremacy of reason, proclaimed as a veritable "dogma", and implying the denial of everything that is of a supra-individual order, notably of pure *intellectual intuition* [and] the exclusion of all true *metaphysical knowledge* [emphases added]' (Guénon, 1945/2004, p. 90). Therefore, rationalism is the very negation of *anemnasis* (νάμνησις), *smriti*, or mindfulness (*sati*), a Platonic 'recollection' toward wisdom and our Buddha-nature. Providing incredibly insight as to why reason succumbs to antihierarchical tendencies—and thus evades transcendence—Wilber (2000) stated the majority of people

> use reason without really knowing the ontogenetic stages that produced it. [It] is simply not immediately obvious to reason that reason itself developed or evolved. [Thus,] the natural stance of reason is to simply assume that it is apart from the world and can innocently reflect on it. (p. 450)

Now the *reflection* paradigm is a legitimate (fifth) stage of consciousness (*fulcrum* or *self-sense*) where the rational-ego (as personal awareness) comprises the language of representation and reflection; unfortunately, as we have already noted, it is a monological representation and *depth*-less reflection concerning a pre-given world and pre-given subject (Wilber, 2000). Equally important is understanding the difference between what Jean Gebser called the mental consciousness crystallising around the time of Plato, Buddha, Laozi, and so on, and its deficient, rational mode. Far from a pinnacle of evolution:

> the rational consciousness is the matrix of scientific materialism, virulent ethnocentrism, terrorism, and existential neuroses. It is a deficient form of consciousness, giving birth to deficient social and cultural manifestations. Far from being the summit of human accomplishment, the rational consciousness is an evolutionary *cul-de-sac*. (Feuerstein, 1992, p. 9)

Similarly, to Shiva (1989)—who argued that modern development is *maldevelopment* —stated that 'activity,[24] productivity, creativity which were associated with the feminine principle are expropriated as qualities of nature and women, and transformed into the exclusive qualities of man. Nature and woman are turned into passive object'[25] (p. 6). While we cannot ascertain the perspective of Shiva, we agree with her wording; we do not see the world as *too masculine* (*yáng*) which is expected from critical, ecological, or feminist angles; rather, the subtlety is that *the male-oriented view has usurped the feminine principle* (Figure 3).

A KALEIDOSCOPIC VIEW OF CHINESE PHILOSOPHY OF EDUCATION

Remarks on Contemplation, Rationality, and Mindfulness

The present antithesis between East and modern West consists (and subsists) 'in the fact that the East upholds the superiority of contemplation over action, whereas the modern West on the contrary maintains the superiority of action over contemplation' (Guénon, 1927/2004, p. 36). Plato would distinguish reason (*ratio*) from contemplation (*contemplatio*; θεωρία, *theōría*; *dhyāna*) as evident by the etymology of philosophy: a 'love of wisdom' cannot be wisdom, but points to a higher, 'non-human' source. Another fundamental difference between East (or traditional West) and modern West is that the former—with the possibility of interior development—attempts to become a higher vestige of one-Self whereas the latter attempts to disprove the highest thinker of one's era. In over 2000 years no one has disproved the Buddha; instead, all sincere aspirants try and reach their Buddha-nature. In the Westernised context, one (often) succumbs to a battle for superiority, a mental jousting of one's own ideologies and prestige; as a result, blatant polemical attacks thoroughly infuse postmodern criticism, slighting the fact that without diverse views there can be no conceptual (or dialogical) growth! Given the spiritual degeneration, however, perennialist Schuon (2001/2007) would speak frankly:

> All civilizations are fallen, but in different ways: the fall of the East is passive; the fall of the West is active. The fault of the fallen East is that it no longer thinks; that of the fallen West is that it thinks too much, and wrongly. The East is sleeping over truths; the West is living in errors. (pp. 17, 18)

In our concern for education, we must address the fundamental duality of contemplation and action as it relates to liberation (*mokṣa*) or transformation of the student. Contemplation, zen, or non-action (*wú wéi*, 无为) corresponds to the heavenly pole and action (*karma*) corresponds to the earthly pole. Staying true to metaphysics, contemplation finds manifestation in action as change finds its superior principle in the unchanging. Moreover, action, 'being merely a transitory and momentary modification of the being, *cannot possibly carry its principle and sufficient reason in itself*; if it does not depend on a principle outside its own contingent domain, it is but *illusion* [emphasis added]' (Guénon, 1927/2004, p. 37). So 'action, no matter of what sort, *cannot* under any circumstances *liberate from action*; in other words, it can *only bear fruit within its own domain*, which is that of human individuality [emphasis added]' (Guénon, 1925/2004, p. 158), or the domain of possibility for agency and communion. So the very *possibility* of action is found in 'contemplation, or, if one will, in [metaphysical] *knowledge*, for these two terms are fundamentally synonymous, or at least coincide, since it is impossible in any way to separate knowledge from the process by which it is acquired' (Guénon, 1927/2004, p. 37). Therefore, metaphysicians are astounded that movement and change (exclusively *yīn*) are actually 'prized for their own sake, and not in view of any end to which they may lead [Being]; this is a direct result of the absorption of all human faculties in outward action whose necessarily fleeting character [implies] dispersion' (1927/2004, p. 38). Herein lies the context for pragmatism, whose action-oriented philosophy sparked both social and educational reform.

Pragmatism has historically substituted *truth* for *utility*—coinciding with *predictive power* (Wilber, 2000)—and the foundational branches of science (and education) essentially became a science of *rocks* (the least in holonic consciousness); 'the "ideal" of [scientific] knowledge as predictive power would ruin virtually every field it was applied to (including rocks) because its very methods would erase any creativity it would find, thus erasing precisely what was novel, significant, valuable, meaningful' (Wilber, 2000, p. 56). While pragmatists are certainly apprehensive of industry and its application in education—arguing for experiential learning against uniformity, standardisation, and a pre-given world—we cannot help but notice both pragmatism and mechanism derive from the same premise of a superiority of action; in seeking to overcome the deficiencies of a "mechanistic" education, has pragmatism inevitably strengthened the very premise of uniformity in curricular standardisation?

Respecting the *yáng*

In a traditional (read: spiritual) approach to education, the disciple aimed to *transcend* the limitation[26] of their lower mind (*xīn*, 心) and general psychosomatic constitution. Unfortunately, a historical precedent was set to abandon the mind and neglect the body in antimaterial spirituality—what we consider legitimately as too *yáng*. In Zen or Chán (禅) Buddhism, one 'stunk of Zen' if unbalanced toward *shén* (神). Nonetheless, each stabilised fulcrum beyond reason is a *trans-rational* contemplative development that may be rationally explained or reconstructed, but never rationally experienced. In transpersonal psychology, the higher fulcrums of awareness are categorised as vision-logic (*centaur*), psychic, subtle, causal, and nondual (Wilber, 2001). Vision-logic is an *integral-aperspectival* mind, adding 'up all the perspectives tout ensemble, and therefore privileges no perspective as final: it is aperspectival' (Wilber, 2000, p. 193). The bodymind holon of the centaur is an intersubjective transcendence from universal perspectivism (rational holon), capable of integrating body and mind: a mind looking at the mind intersubjectively as opposed to operating within the mind alone (reflection paradigm). For Gebser, the vision-logic consciousness that surpassed the mental was his *integral consciousness*,

> associated with ego-transcendence (rather than egolessness), self-transparency, freedom from anxiety (especially from the fear of time), openness, emotional availability and fluency, participatory freedom, personal responsiveness, bodily presence (rather than abstraction from life), the ability for genuine intimacy, equanimity, reverence for all life, the capacity for service, and love. (Feuerstein, 1992, p. 19)

Each interior stage of consciousness has an exterior correlate (Figure 2).[27] According to Wilber (2001), a centaur uses hermeneutic (*interior*) depth (dialectical and dialogical) and (*exterior*) developmental (evolution and network) languages. The *psychic* begets inner vision and exterior vibration (of intensity, not physics). The subtle domain exemplifies the *saint* comprising inner luminosity and outer Platonic archetypes. The causal-level exemplifies the *sage* who recognises the emptiness behind the great dream (*māyā*) and dancing play (*līlā*) of manifestation. And the language of the

A KALEIDOSCOPIC VIEW OF CHINESE PHILOSOPHY OF EDUCATION

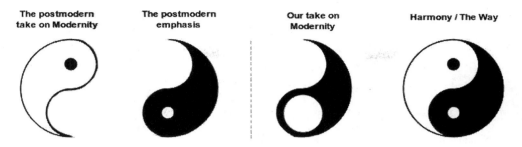

Figure 3: Differences in unbalanced worldviews on modernity through the perspective of Daoist imagery

Notes: The postmodernist view en-visions modernity as too *yáng* whereas we see it as too *yáng-in-yīn* based on the subtle nature of the collapse of the *yáng* to the *yīn* (Figure 1); thus, the *yáng* was left to assume the position of the *yīn*. In this conceptual map, we contextualise both Figures 1 and 2 and the subtle reductionism inherent in translative movements mistaken for authentic spiritual transformation. The lack of discernment between uniformity and unity, as well as a 'more-than-human' biosphere is also encompassed in our take on modernity. If the absurdity of the symbol is in question, so too, we argue, is the lack of discernment in the aforementioned paradoxes that result from a lack of depth and genuine contemplation.

nondual is the extraordinary ordinary, where interior and exterior are One in the *siddha*.

Now the triumphant return of the (balanced) feminine principle—at least academically—has been to the detriment and omission of its *yáng* or masculine counterpart. Naturally, one cannot conceive of a purely *yīn* universe and concede *yáng* entirely, nor a dichotomy of *yīn* and *yáng*; however, in a theologically or metaphysical context, we have left Heaven (*yáng*) for Earth (*yīn*). Should we tend solely toward the needs inherent in the material side of our nature, the aim becomes 'quite *illusory* since it constantly *creates more artificial needs than it can satisfy* [emphases added]' (Guénon, 1927/2004, p. 17). Therefore, despite theoretically removing the *yáng-in-yīn* imbalance from modernity—to which we applaud—we are left spirituality impoverished with the integrative absence of *involution* (*yáng* tendency).

Concluding Remarks

To summarise mindfulness—the foundation of contemplation—we present the phrase 意念 (*yì niàn*) or 'wisdom mind-thought.' The Chinese character *niàn* 念 is comprised of *jīn* (今) 'now; this' and *xīn* (心) 'heart; mind' which captures the moment-to-moment awareness which manifests a state of here-and-now oneness through embodied engagement (Lu, 2012). Together, 意念 relates the wisdom mindfulness is oriented toward. And according to Wallace (2006), contextualising mindfulness practice toward mental balance (*samādhi*) includes attention (*śamatha*), contemplative insight (*vipaśyanā*), and the cultivation of the four immeasurables: loving-kindness (*metta*), compassion (*karuṇā*), empathetic joy (*muditā*), and equanimity (*upekṣā*). In the Indo-Tibetan context, one does not refrain 'from labelling or categorising experiences in a nonjudgmental fashion;[28] [instead] in the earliest, most authoritative accounts, *sati* is said to distinguish between wholesome and unwholesome, beneficial and unbeneficial tendencies. The contrast between the ancient and modern accounts is striking' (p. 61).

A KALEIDOSCOPIC VIEW OF CHINESE PHILOSOPHY OF EDUCATION

Having presented the foundations for the traditional practice(s) of mindfulness, we hope our contextual efforts and conceptual map (Figure 3) aid pedagogical theorists toward qualifying a mindful education embracing Eastern wisdom. Further education research may elucidate mindfulness toward the integral-aperspectival mind, so long as the *yáng* (spiritual) element is in continual balance with the *yīn*, and vice versa.

Disclosure statement

No potential conflict of interest was reported by the authors.

Notes

1. In a Qigong context, we note Yang's (1997) use of the word *yi* (意) meaning the mind related to clear thinking, judgment, and wisdom.
2. Following Wilber (2000), we leave Nature (environment) capitalised to distinguish between human nature and metaphysical NATURE (Figure 1).
3. To Shiva (1989), *subject-less knowledge* creates a *dichotomy*; the 'fact-value dichotomy is a creation of modern reductionist science, while being an epistemic response to a particular set of values, *posits itself as independent of values* [emphasis added]' (pp. 26, 27): a paradox of relativism.
4. A Latin, theological phrase meaning 'in the aspect of eternity.'
5. c.f. *On metaphysics and the possibility of integration*; we denote what is fixed (as permanence) as too *yáng*-in-*yīn* and its metaphysical counterpart, *stasis*, as *yáng*. See also Appendix A.
6. A term in contrast to *dia*logical and *trans*-logical. Monological investigation implies theorising on what we observe through our senses and subsequent extensions.
7. An analysis of the manifold application of the tool vs. the machine is beyond the scope of our paper. However, we wish to expound that uniformity is in no way too *yáng* in contrast to diversity or *yīn*; rather, it results from a worldview with too *yáng*-in-*yīn* (Figure 3).
8. More qualifiers exist, but disciple in particular is of two forms: outward, often associated with a religious West, and inward, often associated with a meditative East.
9. This would imply that science taught in education is unreliable at worst, and generally oversimplified at best; and any systemisation leads to exclusion: a topic beyond the scope of our paper.
10. The Daoist scholar would have little issue with this paradox as *yīn* is within *yáng* and *yáng* within *yīn*.
11. It is prudent to note that horizontally, agency relates to the masculine (*yáng*) and communion relates to the feminine (*yīn*). However, in the vertical context (Figure 2), these earthly *yīn* and *yáng* movements are *yīn* in relation to the vertical *yáng* archetype of Spirit or *shén*.
12. An inversion where *yáng* is now situated in *yīn*, hence too *yáng*-in-*yīn*.
13. Also known as vitalistic intuition.
14. The exception being esoteric currents of pre-Pauline Christianity.
15. In Buddhist China. *avidyā* (无知, ignorance, suffering; Tibetan: *ma rigpa*) is the first of twelve chains or causes (*nidānas*) applicable to *pratītyasamutpāda* ('dependent origination' or 'interdependent co-arising') and connects with suffering (*duḥkha*) or unsatisfactoriness (Tibetan: *sdug bsngal*).
16. The 'double truth' in Buddhism: one relative and conventional, the other absolute and certain (Coomaraswamy, 1947).
17. Or *substance* in Scholastic terminology, from *sub-stare*, 'that which stands beneath.'
18. Or *essence* in Scholastic terminology.
19. Rather than 'dualism' which is necessarily a 'naturalism' if conceived as being irreducible.
20. Unfortunately, such symbolism has historically manifested as patriarchal systems. We are certainly not against these many critical, feminist, and deep ecological criticisms. We simply

allude to the fact that these two tendencies are found within all manifested reality to such and such a degree.
21. Like mindfulness, Qigong as a hierarchical practice is extracted and abstracted from the sequence Wàigōng 外功 (External Work), Nèigōng 内功 (Internal Work), Qìgōng 气功 (Energy Work), and Shéngōng 神功 (Spirit Work).
22. To his credit, Davis himself is a strong advocate for the *hermeneutic circle* where one places their intersubjectivity at face value to contextualise and transcend. Without his formulations on educational complexity and deep ecology, we would not have had the opportunity to write and present our own thesis.
23. While we cannot address the intricacies of *Meno*, we assume the spiritual process Plato described was *exosomatosis*.
24. If we remain strictly with Daoist teachings, we note that the masculine principle is *active* and the feminine principle *passive*. Here *activity* as a noun should be replaced with *action* which has its proper correlation with *contemplation* which is truly *active*. A better descriptor would be *movement*.
25. In a similar vein, the *subjugated subjects* (*biopower*) of Michel Foucault and *dehumanising humanism* of Jürgen Habermas concerned a collapse of *dia*logical subjects into *mono*logical objects: a *pseudo-science* based on 'self-aggrandizing *power*' (Wilber, 2000, p. 464).
26. If the mental faculty was not limited, what need would anyone have in transcending it?
27. This is why mindfulness can be measured as brain waves.
28. As seen in Western mindfulness deriving from Western psychology.

ORCID

Chunlei Lu http://orcid.org/0000-0002-8623-0274

References

Bowers, C. (2010). Toward an eco-justice pedagogy. *Environmental Education Research, 8,* 21–34.

Blom, R., Lu, C., & Mgombelo, J. (2015). Mindful pedagogy: Invocating the concept of play beyond the confines of recess. *Paideusis: Journal of the Canadian Philosophy of Education, 22,* 38–49.

Capra, F. (1997). *The web of life: A new scientific understanding of living systems.* New York, NY: Anchor.

Coomaraswamy, A. K. (1947). *Time and eternity*. Ascona: Artibus Asiae.
Coomaraswamy, A. K. (1987). *Metaphysics*. Princeton, NJ: Princeton University Press.
Davis, B. (2004). *Inventions of teaching: A genealogy*. Mahwah, NJ: Lawrence Erlbaum.
Feuerstein, G. (1992). *Wholeness or transcendence? Ancient lessons for the emerging global civilization*. Burdett, NY: Larson Publications.
Guénon, R. (1924/2004). *East and west*. (M. Lings, Trans.). Hillsdale, NY: Sophia Perennis.
Guénon, R. (1925/2004). *Man and his becoming according to the Vedānta* (R. Nicholson, Trans.). Hillsdale, NY: Sophia Perennis.
Guénon, R. (1927/2004). *The crisis of the modern world* (R. C. Nicholson, A. Osborne, & M. Pallis, Trans.). Hillsdale, NY: Sophia Perennis.
Guénon, R. (1945/2004). *The reign of quantity and the signs of the times* (L. Northbourne, Trans.). Hillsdale, NY: Sophia Perennis.
Guénon, R. (1946/1991). *The great triad* (P. Kingsley, Trans.). Ghent, NY: Sophia Perennis.
Guénon, R. (1946/2004). *Perspectives on initiation* (H. D. Fohr, Trans.). Ghent, NY: Sophia Perennis.
Lodewyk, K., Lu, C., & Kentel, J. (2009). Enacting the spiritual dimension in physical education. *The Physical Educator, 66*, 170–179.
Lu, C. (2012). Integrating mindfulness into school physical activity programming. *Teaching and Learning, 7*, 37–46.
Schuon, F. (1970/2009). *Logic and transcendence: A new translation with selected letters* (M. Perry, J. Lafouge, & J. S. Cutsinger, Trans.). Bloomington, IN: World Wisdom.
Schuon, F. (2001/2007). *Spiritual perspectives and human facts* (M. Perry, J. Lafouge, & J. S. Custinger, Trans.). Bloomington, IN: World Wisdom.
Shiva, V. (1989). *Staying alive: Women, ecology and development*. London: Zed Books.
Smith, D. G. (2006). *Trying to teach in a season of great untruth*. Rotterdam: Sense Publishers.
Toulmin, S. (1990). *Cosmopolis: The hidden agenda of modernity*. Chicago, IL: The University of Chicago Press.
Wallace, B. A. (2006). *The attention revolution: Unlocking the power of the focused mind*. Somerville, MA: Wisdom.
Wilber, K. (2000). *Sex, ecology, spirituality: The spirit of evolution*. Boston, MA: Shambhala.
Wilber, K. (2001). *The eye of spirit: An integral vision for a world gone slightly mad* (3rd ed.). Boston, MA: Shambhala.
Yang, J. (1997). *The root of Chinese qigong: Secrets for health, longevity, & enlightenment*. Wolfeboro, NH: YMAA Publication Center.

A KALEIDOSCOPIC VIEW OF CHINESE PHILOSOPHY OF EDUCATION

Appendix A. Catalogue of terminology

Mindfulness (*yīn-yáng*)	Modern (too *yáng*-in-*yīn*)	(W)holistic (too *yīn*)
Mindbody integration	Mindbody dissociation	Mindbody pre-differentiation
Simple	Complicated	Complexity
Holons	Parts	Wholes
Qualitative superiority	Quantitative superiority	Balance between quantity and quality
Trans-rational	Rational	*Pre*-rational and rational
Kosmic agency-in-communion (enactivism)	Stunted agency (reason only)	Gaian participation (communion)
Supra-human	Infra-human	Human
Eco-noetic	Ego-enlightened	Eco-romantic
Unity in multiplicity	Uniformity	Multiplicity
NATURE	Nature	Nature and nature
Spiritual	Mechanical	Ecological
Metaphysics	Physics	Biology
Integral	Empirical	Phenomenological
Wisdom	Information	Lived experience
Product of the process	Product	Process
Depth (and span)	Span	Span
Knowledge	Known	Knower
Synthesis	Analytical	Systems
Contemplative superiority	Active superiority	Active superiority (pragmatism)
Centaur vision logic	Egoic rationality	Emotions

Translation, the Knowledge Economy, and Crossing Boundaries in Contemporary Education

Yun-shiuan (Viola) Chen

Abstract

Significant developments in the global economy and information technology have been accompanied by a transformation in the nature and process of knowledge production and dissemination. Concepts such as the knowledge economy or creative economy have been formulated to accommodate the new and complex developments in knowledge, creativity, economy, and technology. While much of the current literature on the knowledge and creative economy substantially reflects the economic impact of knowledge and creativity, previous studies have rarely touched upon the role of translation in this development. By discussing the role of translation as a generative process in the creative economy and its implications for crossing boundaries in education, this paper argues that translation plays a significant role in the creation of a hybrid milieu. This dynamic cultural hybridity is stimulated by the circulation of knowledge and information via translation, but is also, per se, *a driver inviting greater engagement of ideas and knowledge given that translated works always require retrospective interpretations along with changing social and cultural mores.*

Introduction

Within the context of globalization, a number of studies have eloquently delineated and characterized different ways in which forces of globalization shape contemporary life (e.g. Appadurai, 1996; Bauman, 1998, 2000; Castells, 1996). Among the many theoretical approaches devoted to understanding globalization, the concept of the creative economy, which involves ideas, arts, knowledge, etc., has gained much currency for educators and policy-makers. Theorists of the knowledge and creative economy have described the increasingly significant interconnectedness of knowledge, information technology, and economic development on the global scale. The increasing significance of these theories is also intimately associated with education as means for developing, producing, reproducing, and circulating knowledge. Nevertheless, in the discussion of globalization theories and the global knowledge economy, there seems to be an assumption of universal proficiency in English as a *lingua franca*, while not much discussion focuses on the role of translation (Bielsa, 2005). This scenario reflects Venuti's (1995) cultural criticism that translation has remained transparent and invisible.

This paper is devoted to revealing the interplay between knowledge, translation, and the culturally creative economy in the current global education context. I argue that neglecting the complexity of translation in the discussion of the creative economy and the global knowledge ecology implies, rather unrealistically, a world free of language and cultural differences. This kind of discussion of the knowledge and creative economy could easily fall into the trap of applying claims of universal knowledge to different cultural contexts. Based on views of Walter Benjamin, Paul Ricoeur, and Homi Bhabha that reflect various dimensions of translation, this paper suggests that translation actually plays a stimulating and productive role not only in reflecting the complexity between language and subjectivity, but also in creating a hybrid milieu, which is significant in the development of knowledge and cultural creative economies that are often addressed by educational policy-makers without addressing the many inherent problems. Discussing the role of translation in education, Farquhar and Fitzsimons (2011) draw on several significant philosophers' works to articulate the power of language and of 'translation as a metaphor for education' (p. 652). They maintain that language communicates, by its contingent and arbitrary nature, 'our curse and blessings as part of our ethical endeavor as educators'. This entails the potential of creative dialogs (ibid). Adding to their discussion and the current literature related to knowledge and cultural creative economy, the present paper not only attempts to complicate the role of translation in education settings, but also serves as a critique of the knowledge/cultural creative economy, suggesting that an overemphasis on the economic effect of knowledge dissemination and sharing helps neither educators nor students to appreciate knowledge and the circulation of ideas, nor does it assist in the development of a knowledge/cultural creative economy.

This paper begins by reviewing the leading literature on knowledge, and the creative and knowledge economy in translation. This review is followed by a co-articulation of translation in relation to the unfolding of the creative economy. Moreover, Ricoeur and Bhabha's arguments about translation are discussed, since their intriguing approach to translation reveals the dynamically hybrid milieu produced and engaged by translation. While this hybrid culture as such is induced by translations of all kinds of cultural works, it further stimulates cultural creativity, innovation, and knowledge because of the indefinite and deferred meanings of translated texts. This paper concludes by discussing the implications of translation to the borderlessness in the current educational context.

The significance of this discussion can be viewed according to two perspectives. First, it illustrates the invisible but critical role of translation in the knowledge economy and in education. Translation is not only involved in the area of hermeneutic interpretations of different cultures and languages, but also in creative and transformative actions devoted to the circulation and dissemination of knowledge and ideas. These features accord well with the creative economy and its concerns about how ideas propagate and multiply. The fact that the meanings of terms and usages are deferred and differ to various degrees during the process of transformation from one language to another, reveals an inherently dynamic milieu created by translation, requiring further re-reading and re-working. This generative process keeps ideas and knowledge emerging and growing, which further calls into question the conventional and dominant thinking that knowledge can be translated and transmitted in a direct and linear fashion. Given that the emergence and formation of knowledge and ideas are subject to sociocultural conditions, translation requires continuous deliberative retrospection. Second, the understanding of this complexity further calls for a more systematic and critical engagement with translation, knowledge, and translated works in educational settings, in particular when speaking of crossing boundaries in education.

Knowledge, Creative and Knowledge Economy

The concept, definition, and the whole understanding of knowledge *per se* is a broad field of research that has provoked numerous debates for centuries. In what we call epistemology, philosophers have been engaged with issues surrounding the nature, classification, production, circulation, and receptions of knowledge. From the West to the East, from the ancient times to contemporary times, philosophers such as Plato (2013), Bacon (1605), and Kuhn (1962), as well as Confucius (2008) and the Confucian followers that formed a major ruling class in ancient Chinese history, all represent a wide variety of traditions of engaging epistemology. Taking several contemporary philosophical approaches as instances, while positivists such as Auguste Comte argue that authentic knowledge can be found only through a set of 'scientific methods', Max Weber points out the significance of experience and interpretation in knowledge production. Moreover, while a structuralist might consider knowledge as a part of broader social and cultural structure, a post-structuralist may regard knowledge as interrelated discourses driven by various powers and could be complicit with these powers (e.g. Foucault, 1980).

Taking into account historical, sociological, and cultural aspects, discussions of knowledge become even more complicated. For instance, studies in the field of sociology of knowledge, such as those by Mannheim (1929), Berger and Luckmann (1966), Bourdieu (1988), and Burke (2000, 2012), all unveil the dynamisms between sociocultural contexts and practices, historical development, as well as knowledge. They manifest the sociocultural and historical meanings of knowledge that unsettle our perceptions of knowledge as truth, and, to some extent, point to the challenges of translating knowledge that is in fact full of sociocultural meaning. In the same vein, engaging research on knowledge with economic concerns extends the understanding of concepts of knowledge. For instance, the sociohistorian of knowledge, Burke, eloquently demonstrates that the rising of the knowledge class can be traced back as early as to sixteenth century when printing technology came into being along with increasing opportunities in governments and churches for educated knowledge holders to work with their knowledge (2000, pp. 116–148); hence, the commercialization of information and knowledge is as old as capitalism (ibid., pp. 149–176). Nevertheless, terms such as cultural economy, knowledge economy, and creative economy have emerged and thrived recently, illustrating that economic scenarios of creativity and knowledge being used for revenue still catch policy-makers' and educators' attention.

Mindful of these diverse perspectives of knowledge, this paper has no intention to exhaust all of them. For the current purposes, I simply specify that the knowledge and ideas discussed in this paper are defined in a broad way, i.e. systematic information surrounding an object, an issue, or a field. Knowledge and ideas can be subjective or objective, experiential or positivist, including the post-structural thoughts that conceive knowledge as a set of discourse, narratives, or practices interwoven with powers.

Returning to the terms cultural, knowledge, and creative economy, the phrase 'cultural economy' was originally coined by the Frankfurt School philosophers, Adorno and Horkheimer (1944), to criticize the mass production of cultural products such as films and paintings, which were deemed to be employed as tools to serve capitalism. For them, the culture industry creates a sense of false consciousness among the masses and confuses real needs with endless desire. Such confusion further endangers the high culture and art that can meet genuine human needs, such as creativity, freedom, and happiness. From this perspective, the cultural industry can by no means be a real source of genuine creativity and knowledge development. Such critical views, to some extent, reflect the powerful invasion of capitalism into the cultural sphere which could blind the public to their real statuses and needs. Nevertheless, I argue that this notion seems to imply that the public is incapable of reflecting on their actual positions. Such a view underestimates the public's agency. In fact, what they criticized as cultural industry could also be a source of creativity, though this creativity might not be manifested in the ways recognized or appreciated by high cultural classes.

Along with the drastic development of information and communication technology as the driving forces of globalization, since World War II, numerous studies have described and analyzed the emerging economic activities surrounding knowledge and creativity (e.g. Drucker, 1992; Florida, 2002; Machlup, 1962; Stiglizt, 1999). In discussing this trend, Peters (2010) illustrates the three strands of the 'learning economy', 'creative economy', and 'open knowledge economy'. He describes how these terminologies attempt to theorize the knowledge economy, knowledge society, and more importantly, the 'wider and broader changes in the nature of capitalism, modernity, as well as the global economy' (ibid., p. 67). To this can be added the term creative economy, which has arisen quite recently. Peters traces the initial usage of the term to Hawkins (2001) and Florida (2002). The former features creativity from various perspectives of knowledge, the development of creative sectors such as movies, publications, etc., on the global scale, the critical role of technology and management in advancing ideas and creativity to form businesses, and the concept and significance of intellectual property and patents in creative business. Florida refers to the emergence of 'the creative classes' and their activities in various dimensions and illustrates their profound impact in shaping contemporary life. Undoubtedly, the contributions of these theorists lie in their phenomenal identification and delineation of newly emerging economies based on ideas, creativity, and knowledge, i.e. 'the turn from steel and hamburgers to software and intellectual property' (Peters, 2010, p. 71). This set of new discourse is also drawing policy-makers' attention and gradually exerting its influence on education. For instance, the UN's *Creative Economy Reports* (2008, 2010) broadly investigate the multiple dimensions of the creative economy, such as the concepts, context, and promotion of the creative economy, while many Asian governments and educational institutions (e.g. Lai, 2007; Ministry of Education of Taiwan, 2003) also encourage educators to offer creative education classes in response to the creative economy, because education plays such a pivotal role in the supply and quality of knowledge, innovation, and creativity.

Nevertheless, while most research and policy papers have discussed how knowledge and creativity can be highly profitable for businesses, contributing to economic development, and strongly recommend including knowledge transfer, cultivation of creativity, and innovation in education to continuously develop economies, such research and reports have rarely gone beyond the utilitarian view of the role of education in the creative economy. As Peters (2010) notes, much of the literature considers education, training, and skill acquisitions as a part of the creative economy. Educational policies need to encourage a kind of creativity that takes into account not only the role of new social media but also the knowledge ecology that democratizes access to knowledge and decentralizes the structures of knowledge production (ibid., p. 73).

Peters' articulation of the knowledge ecology is more interested in knowledge access and production as well as the potential of new social media. For this paper, his articulation is particularly useful in pointing out the ecological dimensions of how knowledge and ideas are transmitted and disseminated on a global scale. This idea draws our attention to translation as a complex process of production, dissemination, reception, adaption, and application of knowledge and ideas. Neglecting the role of translation in this process not only undermines the validity of these theorists' arguments, but also reflects an implicit English-speaker-centric mindset. In a fundamental sense, knowledge and ideas are produced and emerge in different sociocultural circumstances and need to be translated before they travel to and are adopted in other contexts.

Complexity of Translation

It is commonly agreed that the most fundamental meaning of translation is the transferring of messages in one language to another. This is usually thought to be a fairly simple and straightforward process. This technical and mechanical view of translation is however limited since it focuses solely on the results of translation. The transferring process comprises a series of elements starting with interpreting and grasping signifiers in a language, and locating/inventing another signifier in the targeted language that can appropriately represent what is being signified by the source language. Since language is an essential attribute of cultural signs—including the signifiers and the signified in a culture—translation, in a broad sense, is inherently involved not only in the nature of linguistic meaning but also in cultural interpretation and understanding. The possibility of correct understanding, precise interpretation, and representation of different cultures through various languages requires another space for discussion; for the present discussion, it can be concluded that the role of translation is more complex than the transfer of simplistic vocabulary and messages. Moreover, there are dynamic and productive interrelationships between languages, meaning, culture, as well as various other subjectivities. As Buden and Nowotny (2009, p. 196) eloquently articulate, translation evokes a broad sense of moving or repositioning of linguistic vocabularies, 'human beings', or even properties such as 'cultural and political conditions'.

In this sense, M. Cronin's view also calls attention to the creative cultural and epistemological dimensions of translation by saying that (2003, p. 127):

> Translation as an operation involving two or more languages has *ipso facto* considerable bi-sociative potential ... more time has to be devoted to highlighting the epistemic specificity of translation ... in the concept of distance, the nomadic and the bi-sociative. This emphasis should also include a more comprehensive understanding of the creative nature of the process itself.

This quote similarly points to the needs of unpacking implicit complexity interwoven by threads of language, translation, knowledge, and society that on the surface are the embodiments of these threads and at the same time the inherent constituents driving the productivity of these factors. An omission of the role of translation in the discussion of the knowledge economy neglects the factors of cultural and linguistic diversities and the interaction of their dynamisms with the homogenizing power brought about by globalization. The global phenomenon of English as the *lingua franca*, on the one hand, seems to bridge different cultures; on the other hand, it also creates an illusion that everything can be un-problematically transferred to English and again from English to other languages, or vice versa. This paper further pursues this complexity and its implication by discussing knowledge dissemination and cultural hybridity in education.

Translation and Creativity

A few researchers have addressed issues of creativity, critical acts, and translators' subjectivity in translation activities (e.g. Cappelen, 2008; Loffredo & Perteghella, 2006; Massardier-Kenney, 2010; Munday, 2009). To advance the idea that translation is a stimulus of a broader creative milieu within the knowledge and creative economy, this study borrows Walter Benjamin's inspiring views about translation as a pursuit of pure language in his renowned work *The Task of the Translator* (1923/2004). Benjamin articulates that different languages supplement each other in their intentions. According to Benjamin, 'All supra-historical kinship of languages rests in the intention underlying each language as a whole' (p. 78), because translation reveals different conditions (in various cultures) of a signifier, and, at the same time, the signified becomes more complete. For instance, different societies might all have similar breads that can be described as a 'bun', and translating the signifier 'bun' could reveal various material conditions and economic environments related to 'bun'. Translation therefore approximates the best knowledge about the word 'bun'. Terms describing abstract concepts offer another example. While 'knowledge' in the West usually has empirical and experiential meanings, 'tao' (道), as knowledge and practice, in the Chinese context plays a similar role in intellectual life but oftentimes has strong ethical implications guiding daily practices. By translation, these implications and connotations break the surface of the meaning of the word. As Pym elaborates (2003, p. 100), although there is no way that two different signifiers (from two different cultures) with a similar signified message can be full equivalents, 'the attempt to translate them into each other ... must produce some knowledge not only about the thing they signify, but also about the different modes of signification'. I would argue that the efforts to bridge the gap between these non-full-equivalencies of similar signifiers allow one to see the abundant knowledge surrounding the signifier. This knowledge appears in the attempt at translation and the different modes of signification. This is how translations complicate our knowledge toward an intention, an object, or the domain of a subject, and at the same time, expand and approximate our knowledge.

Benjamin's argument has significant implications for our pondering of creativity in relation to cultural hybridity in two ways. First, at the micro level, it opens a door for us to see the generative process translators engage in by incorporating knowledge and language, as well as their creativity in searching, coining terms, or sometimes even assigning new meanings to terms beyond conventional senses in the target language. Second, at the macro level of creativity, within the grand cultural milieu which is supportive of creativity, one sees the potential needs for knowledge to become complete and ideas to become generative in translation, since language, *per se*, as a carrier of knowledge approximates the complete and true picture of the world via translation. In particular, given that languages change and evolve in different time-space contexts, the attempt at translating a body of knowledge produced within a cultural context to a more diverse context requires not just translation, but also continuously retrospective scrutiny of translations. All these efforts enrich and testify to knowledge translated from other cultures. However, in saying this, I do not intend to imply that a body of knowledge, a book, or a text becomes complete or true once it is translated into another language. What is true rather, is that since translated works are generative and productive, they become the stimulus of a creative milieu that could invite and inspire further engagement of invention and creativity for the purpose of unfolding and expanding knowledge.

Ricoeur on the Hermeneutics of Translation

Discussing the micro dimension of productivity in translation in the process of knowledge and idea transfer, Ricoeur's phenomenal work *On Translation* (2006) similarly recognizes the complexity of translation and further places translation within a model of hermeneutic philosophy. His advancement allows us to see the interplay between knowledge, understanding, interpretation, and reconstruction in the process of translation, which is particularly critical in education since it suggests a consideration of multiple interpretations and readings in knowledge translation. When talking about crossing borders in education, without this understanding, one could easily forget the homogenizing power of knowledge even when it in fact originates from within a particular sociocultural context. This should be considered carefully when translating knowledge into other cultural contexts.

Ricoeur discusses translation in terms of two main paradigms: linguistic and ontological. The latter is a new addition to the long tradition of thought about translation in the West (Kearney, 2006, p. xii). In what Kearney called 'the hermeneutic twist', the ontological paradigm of translation directs one's attention toward translation from a pure linguistic level to a more complex level of hermeneutics related to translators' subjectivity. This focus shift further raises questions about the relationships between language, human thought, and the process of individual translation, i.e. how individuals adopt and respond between different cultures embodied in languages.

Following Steiner's *After Babel*, Ricoeur reminds us that cultural difference, manifested in linguistic difference, results in translation. During the translation process, translators work through languages and meaning, serving as a double intermediator between two masters—an author and a reader, as well as a self and an *other*. To bridge and negotiate between the foreign and the home, translation has to deal with understanding, adjustment, and reconstruction. To shorten the distance between the foreign and the home, experienced translators 'reduce the otherness of the other' when translating a work, which also implies the sacrifice of 'one's language claims to self-sufficiency'. (Kearney, 2006, p. xvi) The process of giving up some self-sufficient claims and negotiating to fit oneself into stranger's shoes at the same time allows one to see oneself better, since this sacrifice requires comprehension, comparison, rewording, and reconstructing of the other into oneself and vice versa. Therefore, an appropriate translation needs not only a great degree of openness, but also a particular degree of self-expropriation. For Ricoeur, in both the linguistic and ontological paradigms, 'the task of outer translation finds echoes in the work of inner translation' (ibid., p. xix). To this end, the ethics of translation inherently reflect what Ricoeur calls an interlinguistic hospitality, a critical element making up his ontological paradigm of translation.

By drawing on Ricoeur's argument, this paper does not imply that translating knowledge and ideas is impossible, rather it intends to point out the subtle and dynamic interaction between the outer vs. inner translation and the translation of the foreign vs. the home. This understanding encourages us to reconsider the dissemination of knowledge and ideas in the knowledge economy because knowledge translation is never linear. Most importantly, knowledge translation and ideas generation are deeply involved in a hermeneutic sense of understanding, i.e. understanding oneself and the other while translating the other and oneself, in both linguistic and ontological senses. To put it another way, to translate is to understand, and 'to understand is to translate' (Ricoeur, 2006, p. 24). The hermeneutic model of translation requires educators and policy-makers to deepen their thinking when pondering the application of the knowledge/cultural creative economy to education in relation to translation and advocating education without boundaries.

Cultural Translation, Cultural Hybridity, and the Knowledge Economy

To further the discussion of creativity, knowledge dissemination, and a hybrid cultural milieu in a knowledge/cultural creative economy, we should by no means skip cultural translation theory, which also sheds light on this subject. Cultural translation theory takes a broader approach, suggesting that once one starts to regard translation as a process, one will see that the translation process is nearly omnipresent. For instance, Paz points out how the world is constructed by texts (1992, p. 154, cited from Bassnett & Trivedi, 1999, p. 3). Due to the features of language, texts are always in translation. In a strict sense, no texts can stay in their original form without any change in their application. Accordingly, texts (or signs) are always translated from other texts (or signs). Pym states that, 'Any use of language (or semiotic system) that rewords or reworks any other piece of language (or semiotic system) may be seen as the result of a translational process' (2003, p. 150). This broad sense of translation goes beyond (written and spoken) texts and manifests its particular significance by pointing to a dynamic and constantly generative space of translation which becomes even more vibrant and complex along with the forces of globalization.

One major source of the cultural translation approach is drawn from postcolonial theories. Given that postcolonial theory is actually hotly debated terrain in and of itself (Hall, 2006; Shohat, 1997), it is not difficult to understand that researchers who draw insights from postcolonial theories might have different and sometimes even argumentative perspectives toward translation. For instance, while Niranjana (1992), taking a similar approach to Said's discussion of Orientalism in colonial literature, maintains that translations renew and perpetuate colonial domination (p. 3), Bhabha illustrates a hybrid space between cultures. Although I would not disagree with Niranjana's argument about the potential of translation to promote Orientalism, this argument is less concerned about colonial subjectivities that are reflected in a subtly non-transitive and indirect sense. As von Flotow indicates in her discussion of the perception of receiving cultures toward translated literatures (2007), the process and the outcomes of the literature and the inherent representation of the colonized 'depends as much if not more on the participation and choices of the receiving culture' (p. 187). Voices of the receiving cultures of translated works exist irrespective of whether they are adequately reflected. In particular, translators and the translated work in fact form a hybrid space full of voices of the original authors and the translators.

In this regard, Bhabha's notion of cultural hybridity provides a more nuanced set of lenses by which to scrutinize translation as a hybrid space. In discussing colonial subjectivity, Bhabha (2004) addresses the resistance of the colonized to colonials in their hybrid in-betweenness. Postcolonial hybridity is a survival strategy. Bhabha suggests that borders, which used to be conceived of as rigidly clear and fixed, are blurred everywhere within and between different cultures. Subjectivity is rarely fixed, but fluid and situational. Translators are actually situated in borders between different cultures, where they are in fact indeterminate and constantly transformative. In this sense, 'translation is a performative nature of cultural communication' (ibid., p. 326). Translation is thus not entirely translatable. Consequently, translated works are always waiting and searching for more engagement with understanding, interpretation, and re-translation as they go through various time-space and sociocultural contexts.

Bhabha's major interest lies in the complex subjectivities within colonial contexts and as such, his concept of translation is not limited to its linguistic sense. Nevertheless, his notion of translation in a broad sense is particularly useful to our understanding of cultural translation in relation to the borders of education, knowledge, and the creative economy within the context of globalization. Since 'borders' are everywhere but are at the same time constructed, and therefore can be situational and blurry, it is insufficient to understand knowledge as being translated, transformed, and transited across educational borders in their original sense. Given that knowledge is embodied and constructed by languages, any translation of knowledge inevitably faces the kinds of situations discussed by Benjamin, Ricoeur, and Bhabha, namely that translated knowledge enters into a condition of indefiniteness and uncertainty. This however does not imply translating knowledge is futile or impossible. Cronin spells out in his discussion of translation as a *Doubleness* in relation to globalization and homogenization (2003, pp. 128–131). Thanks to translators, there are simulacrums of these 'economically and culturally powerful originals'. However, these translated copies can only be copies, and, as Cronin indicates, 'The attempt to create a true likeness can only succeed if it fails. The incompleteness of any translation is the very principle of its future creativity' (ibid., p. 131).

To sum up, the cultural translation approach provides the possibility of seeing the ways in which translation can be a driver of cultural hybridity. Since this hybridity is in a condition of incompleteness and is not static like a period, but dynamic like a dash, it opens and provokes creative and innovative engagement. This hybridity could be an implicit driver of the knowledge and creative economy. This perspective further provides significant implications for pondering the dissemination and circulation of translated knowledge as it crosses borders.

Knowledge, Translation, and Education across Borders

Based on the discussions above, this paper draws two implications for thinking about knowledge circulation in the broad sense of education that crosses boundaries. The first is an appeal for adequate and deliberative reconsideration of knowledge translation. The second is that viewing translated knowledge in a different way allows one to advocate diversifying the subjects and linguistic space of education as a translation strategy to generate hybrid open space which can stimulate more knowledge, innovation, and creativity.

By arguing for a more appropriate reconsideration of the knowledge translated in educational settings, this paper calls for more sensitive and open consideration when reading and interpreting translated knowledge by being mindful of the complexity of knowledge translation in today's context of globalization. To make texts meaningful in the sociocultural contexts of target languages, translations from source to target languages need to take into account what Shan Te-hsing (2009) calls 'double contexts of translation'. The meaning and application of knowledge must be engaged by looking into the contexts in which the knowledge is generated. In this process, translated knowledge can be reflected, re-interpreted, and discussed. Just as Ricoeur has reminded us, good knowledge translation by nature is a hermeneutic process that requires interlinguistic and intersubjective hospitality. This process, even though it can only be tentative and full of tension and anxiety, leads to the generation of further knowledge and creativity. Accordingly, this paper suggests not only re-considering the meaning of translation for education, but also integrating and developing a cautious and reflective reading of translated works for educational purposes. By doing so, translation can assist in creating a hybrid and dynamic cultural space in education for the generation of knowledge and ideas.

Secondly, in a more strategic sense, we should look at translation as 'a way of thinking about internationalization' in education (Harris, 2009, pp. 223–233), given that languages constitute us and language translation has to do with the nature of meaning. Meaning has been and must remain a central concern of education. Consequently, enriching linguistic and cultural diversities of student bodies at schools allows more possibilities for creating a hybrid space. Knowledge and subjects in this kind of space can then be translated, generated, and stimulated in a continuously evolving fashion via re-reading, re-interpretation, and re-translation.

Along with globalization, raising multicultural awareness and advocating intercultural dialogs has already been an important goal in education. However, translation in micro (linguistic and individual) and macro (cultural and societal) senses still seems to remain invisible in the field of education. For instance, although reading translated books or academic journal articles is a common practice in higher education and recruiting international students to enrich the student body is also an important policy measure, very few education practitioners, researchers, and policy-makers take into account issues involved in translation as well as its inherent contribution to creating a cultural hybrid environment supporting creativity and knowledge dissemination and production. Being mindful of the role of translation allows educators and students who do not cross physical borders to remember that they in fact have traversed invisible borders with translators in a non-conventional sense whenever they read a translated book, or encounter non-native speakers. Reading translated books actively and critically could be knowledge-generative and educative when crossing these invisible borders.

Conclusion

As forces of globalization have exerted profound influence on contemporary life in many ways, analyzing translation in today's contexts 'allows us to conceptualize and empirically assess how cultural difference is negotiated under globalization and how present trends toward cultural homogenization … are mediated at the local level through strategies of domestication and hybridization' (Bielsa, 2005, p. 143). Further research is needed to address issues related to the role of translation in cultural homogenization. Nevertheless, educational scenarios of crossing boundaries such as immigrant students, international students, visiting scholars, and translated academic books and novels, as well as online learning, have compelled students and teachers to confront an education setting full of visible and invisible boundary crossing. These scenarios, to various extents, all bring in information and knowledge about other cultures. Mindfulness of the delicate process of translation allows one to see the generative and productive features of knowledge.

This paper discusses and argues for the critical role of translation in the knowledge and cultural creative economy in relation to the current educational context. By shifting the focus and viewing translation as a hermeneutic and generative process, we can view translation as a dynamic condition that can further drive greater engagement with knowledge and creativity. Whether or not educational borders are constructed or situational, translation always plays a significant role. Thus, educators should pay more attention on the role translation plays within today's context of globalization.

Acknowledgment

An initial version of this article was presented on the 2012 PESA Conference in Taiwan. I would like express my sincere gratitude to the commentators on the conference and the anonymous reviewers of the journal for their time, insights, and expertise to comment on the earlier version of the article.

Disclosure statement

No potential conflict of interest was reported by the author.

References

Adorno, T., & Horkheimer, M. (1944). *The culture industry: Enlightenment as mass deception.* Retrieved from http://www.marxists.org/reference/archive/adorno/1944/culture-industry.htm

Appadurai, A. (1996). *Modernity at large: Cultural dimension of globalization.* Minneapolis, MN: The University of Minnesota.

Bacon, F. (1605). The advancement of learning. Retrieved from http://www.gutenberg.org/dirs/etext04/adlr10 h.htm

Bassnett, S., & Trivedi, H. (1999). Introduction: Of colonies, cannibals and vernaculars. In S. Bassnett & H. Trivedi (Eds.), *Post-colonial translation: Theory and practice* (pp. 1–18). New York, NY: Routledge.

Bauman, Z. (1998). *Globalization: The human consequence.* Oxford: Polity Press.

Bauman, Z. (2000). *Liquid modernity.* Malden, MA: Polity Press.

Benjamin, W. (1923). The task of the translation: An introduction to the translation of Baudelaire's tableaux parisiens. (H. Zohn, Trans.). In L. Venuti (Ed.), *The translation studies reader* (pp. 75–85). New York, NY: Routledge.

Berger, P., & Luckmann, T. (1966). *The social construction of reality: A Treatise in the sociology of knowledge.* New York, NY: Anchor Books.

Bhabha, H. (2004). *The location of culture.* London: Routledge.

Bielsa, E. (2005). Globalisation and translation: A theoretical approach. *Language and Intercultural Communication, 5*, 131–144.

Bourdieu, P. (1988). *Homo academicus.* Stanford: Stanford University Press.

Buden, B., & Nowotny, S. (2009). Cultural translation: An introduction to the problem, and responses. *Translation Studies, 2*, 196–219.

Burke, P. (2000). Controlling knowledge: Churches and states. In P. Burke (Ed.), *A social history of knowledge: From Gutenberg to Diderot* (pp. 116–148). Malden, MA: Blackwell Publishers.

Burke, P. (2012). *A social history of knowledge II: From the Encyclopedia to Wikipedia*. Malden, MA: Polity Press.
Cappelen, H. (2008). The creative interpreter: Content relativism and assertion. *Philosophical Perspectives, 22*, 23–46.
Castells, M. (1996). *Rise of network society*. Oxford: Blackwell.
Confucius. (2008). *The Analects of Confucius: A philosophical translation*. New York, NY: The Random House Publishing Group.
Cronin, M. (2003). *Translation and globalization*. New York, NY: Routledge.
Drucker, P. (1992). *The age of discontinuity: Guidelines to our changing society*. Piscataway, NJ: Transaction Publishers.
Farquhar, S., & Fitzsimons, P. (2011). Lost in translation: The power of language. *Educational Philosophy and Theory, 43*, 652–662.
Florida, R. (2002). *The rise of the creative class: And how it's transforming work, leisure, community and everyday life*. New York, NY: Basic Books.
Foucault, M. (1980). *Power/knowledge: Selected interviews and other writings, 1972–1977*. New York, NY: Pantheon Books.
Hall, S. (2006). When was the "post-colonial"? Thinking at the limit. In I. Champbers & L. Curti (Eds.), *The post-colonial question* (pp. 242–260). New York, NY: Routledge.
Harris, S. (2009). Translation, internationalisation and the university. *London Review of Education, 7*, 223–233.
Hawkins, J. (2001). *The creative economy: How people make money from ideas*. New York, NY: Penguin Books Limited.
Kearney, R. (2006). Introduction: Ricoeur's philosophy of translation. In P. Ricoeur (Ed.), *On translation* (pp. vii–xx). New York, NY: Routledge.
Kuhn, T. S. (1962). *The structure of scientific revolutions*. Chicago, IL: University of Chicago Press.
Lai, R. (2007). *From creative industries to creative economy: The role of education*. Hong Kong: The University of Hong Kong.
Loffredo and Perteghella. (2006). *Perspectives on creative writing and translation studies*. New York, NY: Continuum.
Machlup, F. (1962). *The production and distribution of knowledge in the United States*. Princeton, NJ: The Princeton University Press.
Mannheim, K. (1929). *Ideology and utopia: An introduction to the sociology of knowledge*. New York, NY: Harcourt, Brace.
Massardier-Kenney, F. (2010). Antoine Berman's way-making to translation as a creative and critical act. *Translation Studies, 3*, 259–271.
Ministry of Education of Taiwan. (2003). *White paper on creative education*. Taipei: MOE.
Munday, J. (2009). The creative voice of the translator of Latin American literature. *Romance Studies, 27*, 246–258.
Niranjana, T. (1992). *Siting translation: History, post-structuralism, and the colonial context*. Berkeley, CA: California University Press.
Paz, O. (1992). Translations of literature and letters. In R. Schulte & J. Biguenet (Eds.), *Theories of translation from Dryden to Derrida* (pp. 152–163). Chicago, IL: University of Chicago Press.
Peters, M. A. (2010). Three forms of the knowledge economy: Learning, creativity and openness. *British Journal of Educational Studies, 58*, 67–88.
Plato. (2013). *Theaetetus*. Retrieved from http://plato.stanford.edu/entries/plato-theaetetus/
Pym, A. (2003). *Exploring translation theories*. Abingdon: Routledge.
Ricoeur, P. (2006). *On translation*. (E. Brennen, Trans.). New York, NY: Routledge.
Shan, T. S. (2009). *Translations and contexts*. Taipei: Bookman Publications.
Shohat, E. (1997). Notes on the post-colonial. In P. Mongia (Ed.), *Contemporary postcolonial theory: A reader* (pp. 322–334). New York, NY: Arnold.

Stiglizt, J. E. (1999). Knowledge as a global public good. In I. Kaul, I. Grunberg, & M. A. Stern (Eds.), *Global public goods: International cooperation in the 21st century* (pp. 308–325). New York, NY: Oxford University Press.
United Nations. (2008). *Creative economy report.* Retrieved from http://unctad.org/en/Docs/ditc20082cer_en.pdf
United Nations. (2010). *Creative economy report.* Retrieved from http://unctad.org/es/Docs/ditctab20103_en.pdf
Venuti, L. (1995). *The translators' invisibility: A history of translation.* New York, NY: Routledge.
von Flotow. (2007). Revealing the "soul of which nation?" Translated literature as cultural diplomacy. In P. St. Pierre & P. C. Kar (Eds.), *In translation – Reflection, refractions, transformation* (pp. 187–200). Amsterdam: John Benjamins Publishing Company.

Index

Notes: Page numbers in *italics* refer to figures
Page numbers in **bold** refer to tables
Page numbers followed by 'n' refer to endnotes

Abram, D. 4
Act to Constitute New Schools 16
Act to Constitute the Imperial University 16
Adorno, T. 91
After Babel (Steiner) 95
Americanisation 10
Ames, Roger 41, 45
Analects 3, 43, 48
Apple, Michael W. 23

Bacon, F. 90
Baumer, Christoph 24
Benjamin, Walter 89, 93, 94, 97
Berger, P. 90
Bhabha, Homi 89, 96, 97
biospherical egalitarianism 63
blackboard: calligraphy, elegant 53–4, 57; writing 53
Blom, Rob 4, 5, 70
Bourdieu, P. 90
Boxer Indemnity Scholarship 15
Boxer protocol 15
Boxer Rebellion 15
Boyd, Michael 8
Buddhism 1, 2, 66, 67; conception of clear mind for developing ecological self 64–5
Burke, P. 90

calligraphy, elegant blackboard 53–4, 57
Capra, F. 72
Cartesian–Newtonian (mechanical) notion 79
CHC *see* Confucian heritage cultures (CHC)
Chen-Yu Lo 17
China: education system 50; government study-abroad scholarships 12–16; identity 29; modern education system, Westernisation of 16–17; modernisation 8, 9, 15; modernisation reforms 9; modern journey of learning from West 9–12; new education system 14; Republican revolution in 14; scholarships 14; students, countries chosen for study abroad 14; Westernisation Movement in 17, 18; Western learning in 16
China-born philosophy 1
China–Britain interactions 13
China-West interactions, histories of 7–9
Chinese philosophy: domain of 2; of education 2, 5
Chou, Y.-W. 8
Chung Ti Shi Yong 17
collaboration 40–3
communication 40–3
Confucian 48; classics 3; creativity 44; framework 42
Confucian heritage cultures (CHC) 1
Confucianism 1, 4, 10, 17, 41
Confucian philosophy 4, 39–41, 43–5
Confucius 40–1, 90; models 43; 'openness to fresh ideas' 43–4
Confucius: Philosopher of Twenty-First Century Skills (Tan) 3–4
consumerism 62
contemplation 81–2
Contextualising Postmodernity in Daoist Symbolism 4
cosmos *vs.* (Pythagorean) Kosmos 76, *76*
costume 26
Creative Economy Reports 92
creativity 43–5; translation and 93–4
A Critical History of Chinese Higher Education 49
critical thinking 38–40
Cronin, M. 93, 97
cultural hybridity 95–7
Cultural Revolution 4, 48, 50
cultural translation 95–7; theory 95–6

INDEX

Daoism 1, 2, 4; imagery *83*; philosophies 4; symbolism 71, 78; theory 73
Davis, B. 76, 79
Daxue 39
Departure from Asia 10
Devall, B. 64, 67
Dewey, John 51
Diamond Sutra 61, 64
Dorling, Daniel 31

Eco camp 74
ecological self 61, 62–3
Eco-Romantics 73; critique 71
ecosophy 60, 67; Naess's efforts in 61
education: across borders 97–8; central problems of 49–52; China 50; Chinese overseas 12–16; European 10; modern 8
educational discourse 37
educational engagement, for self-realisation 66–7
Ego-Enlightenment thinkers 71
Eight-Alliance Nation War 15
Eight-Nation Alliance War 12, 14–16
elegant blackboard calligraphy 53–4, 57
ethnic identity 24
European education system 10

Fadel, C. 38–40, 43–5
First Opium War 2
Fitzsimons, P. 89
Florida, R. 91
Fu Yan 13, 17

Gang Jian Lüe 48
Gebser, Jean 80, 82
Gestalt ontology 63
globalization 88
Golius, Jacob 8
government, Chinese: study-abroad scholarships 12–16
Gross-Loh, Christine 1
Guattari, Felix 66, 67
Guenon, R. 77–9

Hall, D. 38, 41
Hawkins, J. 91
hierarchy 74–6, 78
higher-order thinking skills 39
Hong Taiji 24
Horkheimer, M. 91
hufuqishe 22
hybridity, cultural 95–7

identification 62–4, 66
identity 3; Chinese 29; ethnic 24
Injustice: Why social inequality persists 31
instrumentalism 62
integral-aperspectival mind 82

integral consciousness 82
integral model, adaptation of 75, *75*
Integrated World Capitalism (IWC) 66
integration, possibility of 75–9
IWC *see* Integrated World Capitalism (IWC)

Japan: development of educational studies in 10; Meiji Restoration 17; modern journey of learning from the West 9–12
Ju-Lun Wu 17

Kant, I. 44
Kearney, R. 95
Kim, H. K. 39
King Wuling of Zhao 3, 22–3; exchanges 27, 28; reform 25; reform in *Shiji* 24; rhetoric 28
Kircher, Athanasius 8
knowledge 97–8; Western, dissemination into China *11*
knowledge economy 95–7
Kosmos *vs.* cosmos (Pythagorean) 76, *76*
Kuan Huang 12
Kuhn, T. S. 90

Lao-Tzu 65
Learning from the Barbarians? (Hektor Yan) 3
Lei, Hong-de 4, 48
Liji 3, 34n3
Li Mu 24
lingua franca 89
Lin, Ren-Jie Vincent 2, 7
Liou, W.-C. 8
Li, X.-S. 8, 9
Lu, Chunlei 4, 5, 70
Luckmann, T. 90

Mannheim, K. 90
Martini, Martino 8
May Fourth Movement (1919) 17
Mead, George Herbert 42
Meiji Restoration 10, 13, 14, 16, 17
Memorandum to Fix the Rules and Regulations for New Schools 16
Mencius 26
Meng-Lin Jiang 17
Mengzi 48
metaphysics 75–9
Middle Kingdom (*zhongguo*) 23, 27
mindfulness 81–3, 87
modern education system, Chinese: Westernisation of 16–17
modernisation, of China 8, 9, 15
modernity, postmodern criticism of 71–3
modern nationalism 31
Mongol Empire 2, 24

Naess, Arne 4, 60; biospherical egalitarianism 63; deep ecological attitude

INDEX

67; ecosophy 67; efforts in ecosophy 61; inquiry 62
National Civil Servant Examination System 16
nationalism, modern 31
Ng Aik Kwang 43
Niranjana, T. 96

Odes 38
ontology, Gestalt 63
On Translation (Ricoeur) 94
Opium War 2, 10, 12, 13, 15, 16
Ornstein, Allan C. 57
overseas education: Chinese Government's policies of 9; Chinese government study-abroad scholarships 12–16

personal teaching style: appropriate analogies 54–5; elegant blackboard calligraphy 53–4, 57; fierce passion 55–6
Peters, M. A. 92
P21 framework 39, 40, 42, 44–6
philosophy *see* Chinese philosophy
philosophy of education 49, 53, 54, 57
Ping-Wen Kuo 17
Plato 41, 79, 81, 90
postcolonial theory 96
postmodern criticism, of modernity 71–3
pragmatism 82
problem-centered design: central problems of education 49–52; specific problems encountered by students 52–3
Problem-centred Design and Personal Teaching Style (Hong-de Lei) 4
Puett, Michael 1
Pym, A. 94, 96

Qian Jia Shi 48
Qing Dynasty 2, 3; government 9

race 3, 30, 31, 33
racism 31
rationalism 80
rationality 81–2
Rattansi, A. 28
Republican revolution, in China 14
Resnick, L. B. 38
Ricci, Matteo 8, 9
Ricoeur, Paul 24, 89, 97; on hermeneutics of translation 94–5
Royal Naval College Greenwich 13
Russell, B. 15

scholarships: Chinese Government 14; study-abroad 16–18; Youguang Tu 54; *see also specific types*
Scholasticism 76
Schopenhauer, A. 44
Scientism 49

Second World War 15
self-consciousness 67
self-deficiency, recognition of 2
self-growth 61
self-love 67
self-realisation 61, 63–4; development 64–5; educational engagement for 66–7; Taoist conception of peaceful mind for 65–6
Shan Te-hsing 97
Shih Hu 17
Shiji 33, 35n5; King Wuling reform in 24; of Sima Qian 22
Shijing 38
Shiva, V. 80
Sima Qian 23, 25; *Shiji* of 22
Sino-British Boxer Indemnity Scholarship 15
Sino-Japanese War 12, 14, 16, 18
skills: collaboration 40; communication 40; twenty-first century 37–46
Slingerland, E. 40
Spencer, Herbert 10
spirituality enhancement 64
Steiner 95
students, specific problems encountered by 52–3; Chinese, countries chosen for study abroad **14**
study-abroad scholarships, Chinese government 16–18; countries chosen by Chinese students **14**; overseas education and 12–16

Tan, Leonard 3–4, 37, 42
Taoism 66, 67; conception of peaceful mind for self-realisation 65–6
Tao Te Ching 65
The Task of the Translator 93
The Path: What Chinese Philosophers Can Teach Us About the Good Life (Puett & Gross-Loh) 1
The Three Ecologies 66
Toulmin, S. 71
Toward Self-Realisation (Chia-Ling Wang) 4
transcendence, contextualising reason and possibility of 79–80
translation 5, 97–8; complexity of 92–3; and creativity 93–4; cultural 95–7; Ricoeur on hermeneutics of 94–5
Translation, the Knowledge Economy, and Crossing Boundaries in Contemporary Education (Chen) 5
Trilling, B. 38–40, 43–5
Tsinghua Scholarship 15

universal perspectivism 74

Venuti, L. 89
vision-logic 82
von Flotow 96

INDEX

Wallace, B. A. 83
Wang, Chia-Ling 4, 5, 60
Wang, I.-W. 8
war 12–16; Eight-Alliance Nation War 15; Eight-Nation Alliance War 12, 14–16; First Opium War 2; Opium War 2, 10, 12, 13, 15, 16; Second World War 15; Sino-Japanese War 12, 14, 16, 18
Warring States period 3
Weber, Max 90
Weiming, Tu 45
Westernisation 10; of China's modern education system 16–17
Westernisation Movement, in China 17, 18
Western thinkers 1
What Knowledge is of Most Worth (Spencer) 10
Why Asians are less creative 43
Wilber, K. 73, 75, 77, 80, 82
Wing Yung 13
wisdom: Eastern 70, 71; mindfulness 83; non-human 79
Wu, M.-Y. 8

Xing-Zhi Tao 17
Xiongnu 24
'Xi Xue Dong Jian', critical reflection on 12

Xu, D. 30
Xunzi 3

Yan, Hektor K.T. 3, 22
Yan Hui 43
yiñ imbalance, conceptual errors and paradoxes of 73–5
Youguang Tu 4, 48, 49; personal teaching style 53–6; philosophy of education 49, 53, 54, 57; problem-centered design 49–53; scholarship 54
Youlan Feng 4, 48–9
Yun-Shiuan (Viola) Chen 5, 88

Zen Buddhism 64
Zhan Guo Ce 27, 33, 35n5
Zhao Cheng 23, 26
Zhi-Dong Zhang 17, 18
zhongguo 26
Zhongshu Qian 12
'Zhong Ti Xi Yong' 3, 18; critical reflection on 12
Zhongyong 39, 45
Zhuangzi 55
Zigong 38–9
Zuozhuan 30